THE BOOK OF
FIVE RINGS
FOR EXECUTIVES

For my friends and fellow warriors:

Frank Raiter, Bill Keppen, Al Lindsey,

Jeff Moller, and Chang Miao.

THE BOOK OF FIVE RINGS FOR EXECUTIVES

MUSASHI'S CLASSIC BOOK OF COMPETITIVE TACTICS

DONALD G. KRAUSE

NICHOLAS BREALEY
PUBLISHING

LONDON

First published in the USA by
Nicholas Brealey Publishing Limited in 1999

36 John Street London WC1N 2AT, UK
Tel: +44 (0)171 430 0224
Fax: +44 (0)171 404 8311

1163 E. Ogden Avenue, Suite 705-229
Naperville
IL 60563-8535, USA
Tel: (888) BREALEY
Fax: (630) 428 3442

http://www.nbrealey-books.com

ISBN 1-85788-134-6

Library of Congress Cataloging-in-Publication Data
Krause, Donald G.
      The book of five rings for executives : Musashi's book of
competitive tactics / Donald G. Krause.
         p.   cm.
      ISBN 1-85788-134-6 (alk. paper)
         1. Executives--Psychology.   2. Competition (Psychology)
3. Swordplay. 4. Martial arts. I. Miyamoto, Musashi, 1584–1645.
Gorin no sho.   II. Title.
HD38.2.K73   1999
658.4'001'9--dc21   98-34041
                                                                 CIP

Printed in Finland by Werner Söderström Oy.

CONTENTS

PREFACE

The Book of Five Rings for Executives is the third volume in a continuing series of books about how businesspeople can compete more effectively. The three books, taken together, present my ideas about business strategy, tactics, and management. I cannot claim to have made millions (yet) with these ideas, but I do believe that people become more productive, successful, and satisfied when they are used.

In many respects and for many reasons, this book was the most difficult to write. Accordingly, I needed more help in completing the task. I particularly want to thank Nick Brealey, my publisher in London, and Jeanne Fredericks, my literary agent in the United States, for their patience with my creative agonies. Authors are lonely, discouraged people at times, and often find themselves wandering in a wasteland of bad ideas and frustrating dead ends.

Don Krause
Naperville, IL
July 1998

PART I
INTRODUCTION

I

THE IMPORTANCE OF
THE BOOK OF FIVE RINGS

Over 350 years ago, in 1643, the greatest samurai
swordsman of his day, Miyamoto Musashi, wrote *The
Book of Five Rings*. Musashi was a wandering duelist
who lived during Japan's early feudal period. Born in
1584, he was an accomplished swordsman and later
founded a school to teach sword fighting. According to
legend, from age thirteen to age twenty-nine, he
defeated 60 men in face-to-face duels. Musashi retired
from sword fighting at the age of thirty. He spent the
last three decades of his life, reportedly unwashed and
unshaven, in a cave (which you can visit even today),
perfecting his philosophy of fighting.

Originally, Musashi wrote the text of *The Book of
Five Rings* as a five-part letter to his followers and students. The ostensible purpose of this letter was to pass
down a summary of his methods for winning sword

fights. At a superficial level, the material is very much a Zen Buddhist martial arts instruction booklet.

But the book is far more than a "how-to" text on killing your opponent with a sword. Musashi's work is still studied by millions of people around the world because it is a uniquely valuable resource for improving competitive performance. Musashi's ideas can genuinely tip the competitive odds in your favor. If you look beneath the surface, a powerful set of principles emerges from the writing. These principles are particularly important for business people who are involved in challenging situations. At a deeper level, Musashi's compact book becomes a practical tool for creating and enhancing competitive success. You and virtually everyone else, regardless of job or profession, face competition of some type everyday; the real question is whether you are prepared for it. Musashi provides the essential preparation.

Musashi tells us that while samurai warriors (like business executives) are expected to face challenges and competition in their lives, so too do merchants, farmers, and craftsmen. He says:

People from all walks of life face the consequences of success and failure every day, whether they are prepared for it or not. The difference between a warrior and an ordinary person is that the warrior intentionally studies how to use men, materials, and weapons to gain power, profit, and prestige. Victory and success are not left to the winds of fate nor the whims of

*others. This is the real importance of learning the path
of competition.*

A basic tenet of the samurai warrior lies in the root
meaning of the word "samurai." It comes from a word
meaning "to serve." Samurai warriors, like Musashi,
served their employers with passionate dedication.
Corporate executives and professionals who compete
for their companies with this level of dedication produce success for everyone.

The nature of business everywhere today is such
that you must constantly be ready to compete for customers, markets, and resources. The book you are
reading, *The Book of Five Rings for Executives*, unlocks
the mind and spirit of the master business competitor
in simple, straightforward terms. It discloses the heart
and soul of success in business. It prepares you to overcome the inevitable and necessary challenges you face
all the time. Using modern terminology and concise
examples, the book gives you a clear explanation of
how you can win in competitive situations by employing the best tactics ever developed. Understanding the
principles revealed here will equip you with a powerful
competitive advantage. You can use this advantage to
gain profit, position, and prestige for your company
and for yourself.

Musashi's book is about winning sword fights
between samurai warriors. There is nothing glamorous about sword fights, except in the movies. They
are very personal and very deadly. But then, there is

nothing glamorous about most of the challenges we face in business either. They, too, have a tendency to get very personal and very deadly (at least to your bottom line or your career). A few tragic miscalculations and you may find yourself in the corporate trash dump. Just like your opponent in a sword fight, your business competitors have real names, real faces, real egos, and real personalities, even if they are partially hidden behind a corporate veil. And they are very much in the game to win. *The Book of Five Rings for Executives* gives every business person immediate and critical leverage in this intensely competitive environment. You have a much better chance of succeeding in the fast-paced, wired world of today if you understand and apply Musashi's principles!

Whether you are matched against a salesperson from a rival company or a fellow employee in the next office, the battle is serious, the outcome important. Business deals are made between people, not between companies. Multinational competition plays itself out in face-to-face discussions and negotiations. In Musashi's time, sword fights ended with one person alive and the other person dead or injured. In modern business, winning these personal competitive battles determines your ultimate level of prosperity and prestige. If your competitor wins, you lose. With Musashi fighting alongside, you have a significantly better chance of coming out on top.

The subject of *The Book of Five Rings* is using powerful competitive tactics to overcome challenges. It is about taking immediate and profitable advantage of competitive situations. It is about winning in the here and now. It is not about developing a personal or corporate strategy. Tactics are different from strategy. Strategy is a longer-term concept, while tactics are more immediate. Strategy is, to a great extent, academic and theoretical; tactics are practical. Businesses and executives can survive and prosper without expressed strategies. But, if businesses do not apply effective tactics on a daily basis, they will not survive for very long. No amount of planning for the next campaign does any good if you and your forces are destroyed in the current one. This does not mean that long-term strategy is not important, particularly as a context for tactics. However, the outcome of most competitive interactions in business life eventually boils down to which person uses the better tactics in the present situation.

Tactics are programs and actions designed to meet particular competitive circumstances. They are based on specific factors and local conditions. Hence, tactics have to do with "taking an appropriate action at an appropriate time," as Musashi puts it. In a business world which changes constantly, selecting good tactics is essential. As you will see in the examples I have provided in later in this introduction and in Part III (Battle Tactics for Business), competitive tactics that have proven effective in bringing victory on the battlefield can be adapted to give you an edge in business, if you understand them properly, and if you apply them correctly.

For Japanese business people, Musashi is an old friend and trusted adviser. His material has, over the centuries, become an important reference. Many of the strategies that have been used so effectively by Japanese executives for the last fifty years come directly from Musashi. His approach was studied and utilized by Japanese samurai warriors during centuries of feudal warfare. The modern Japanese businessman, who can be considered (and probably considers himself) the inheritor of the samurai tradition in Japan, also uses Musashi's approach every day to analyze and resolve competitive situations.

There are many examples — automobiles, film and cameras, electronics and small appliances, office equipment, motorcycles, and heavy equipment, to name a few — of how Japanese companies have used Musashi's ideas to gain economic power in the past 50 years, particularly in the United States. Later in this introduction, I will analyze the tactics employed by the Japanese automobile manufacturers to outmaneuver American car makers and seize a significant portion of the US car market. These tactics are based on seven principles of competitive success.

THE SEVEN PRINCIPLES OF COMPETITIVE SUCCESS

I wrote this book because I wanted to make it easy to grasp Musashi's powerful message. There are several excellent literal translations of *The Book of Five Rings*.

However, the difficulty with the literal translations lies in understanding the meaning and application of the ideas to a modern reader's situation, especially a business situation. Western business executives find this particularly troublesome because, more often than not, they lack specific Japanese historical and cultural information. The reinterpretation in this book is much simpler to understand and use.

The Book of Five Rings for Executives provides the fundamentals of competitive success. More significantly, it trains you to use a competitive sword which is capable of winning in all phases of business. But if you are going to use Musashi's very effective methods for winning in competitive situations, you must grasp the competitive sword by the hilt. You must reach into the heart of Musashi's philosophy and extract its essence. Here is how you can do that. I have divided his teachings into seven simple, straightforward tactical principles. If you take a short time to learn and digest these seven principles, you will quickly master the essence of Musashi's philosophy for developing winning tactics in competitive situations.

PRINCIPLE # 1: ORDERED FLEXIBILITY

The mental image I like to conjure up in connection with Musashi's first principle is that of a warrior holding a sword in both hands over his head. He is patiently observing his opponent, waiting for the conflict to begin. The warrior's posture is neither aggressive nor passive. He is the essence of what I call ordered flexibility. Musashi compares the ideal attitude for executing successful competitive tactics to the nature of water. He says:

Water is both ordered and flexible at the same time. It maintains its own identity, but conforms as necessary to the circumstances around it.

Ordered flexibility is the fundamental philosophical tenet of Musashi's entire approach to winning in conflicts. It embodies preparation, observation, poise, timing, and readiness to act. That is, in this position, the warrior is prepared to do whatever is necessary given the actual situation. He is grounded in the reality of the moment, observant and poised. Yet, he can easily respond to changing circumstances. He does not make up his mind to act until the appropriate time; but, when he does act, he moves decisively.

Musashi makes this observation:

The ideal of ordered flexibility is summed up in the concept of "positioning without position." As soon as your opponent recognizes your tactical approach, he can defeat it. Therefore, excessive order and structure lead to brittleness and defeat. On the other hand, if you have no order whatsoever, you cannot concentrate your resources nor time your actions effectively. This also leads to defeat. Balance order with flexibility. Flow like water around obstacles. Move slowly when conditions are unfavorable; move powerfully when the right course opens up. Everyone knows that water in a stream seeks the sea (water is ordered in its objectives), but who can tell how it will get there (water is flexible in its approach)? Think of winning, not of position.

The objective of ordered flexibility is to allow the warrior to determine the most appropriate opportunity or response in a fight. Or, in other words, if the warrior is ordered and flexible in his approach, he is more likely to focus his tactics on probable areas of success. Focus is like the blade of the sword. It determines the cutting edge of competitive tactics. A sharp focus is a critical aspect of success in competitive situations. No person or company has enough resources to exploit every opportunity or fight every battle. Musashi says:

The ability to focus is your greatest asset in a competitive situation. When you appreciate the power of focus, you will feel the rhythm of your opponent and maintain control of his actions. You will understand his approach and effortlessly defeat him by naturally concentrating your attack in an appropriate place at an appropriate time.

Highly effective business executives use ordered flexibility to focus on markets and battles that their companies can win – and win big. The ideal approach in a sword fight, according to Musashi, is to direct your strongest attacks on your competitor's weakest spots. The idea in business is to direct high-output resources into opportunities which produce the greatest profit for the longest time.

PRINCIPLE # 2: EXECUTION

Ordered flexibility is a necessary precedent to effective execution. Execution, that is action, is the one thing that produces results. Execution creates profit. Execution wins victories. Effective execution consists of taking an appropriate action at an appropriate time. (Note: I use the word "appropriate" rather than "right." The word "right" implies that you can know what the outcomes of your actions will be. There is no way to tell, in the heat of battle, whether the actions you are taking are the "right" actions. General George S. Patton once said: "It is the historians that make generals into geniuses. In the midst of a battle, with all the unknowns and uncertainty present, a general can only do his best based on the information he has at the moment." He also said, "A good idea executed promptly today is worth a dozen perfect ideas executed next week." This statement sums up the essential difference between strategic planning and tactical action.)

The foundation for execution and effective action is training. Musashi says:

Be prepared to act when the opportunity arises. This requires both courage and patience, order and flexibility. The ability to perceive and benefit from the moment of advantage is developed through constant study and practice.

The main themes associated with taking action are summarized in the next five principles: resources, environment, attitude, concentration, and timing. The first letters of these themes form the acronym REACT. Hence, the five REACT principles are the components of an effective action program for managing difficult or challenging circumstances.

PRINCIPLE # 3: RESOURCES

Resources are those assets and skills which each side brings to the conflict. They are the raw material of tactics. In business, resources can include people, plant and equipment, finances, and reputation. In all competitive situations, however, the most critical resource is timely and accurate information.

Musashi advises:

Gather information from every possible source. Leave no stone unturned. Use spies, consultants, informants. Perceiving the enemy's strategy allows you to defeat it. Knowing the enemy's position and movement prevents unpleasant surprises.

Information is the fabric of tactics. You can never know too much about your enemy, yourself, or the situation.

PRINCIPLE # 4: ENVIRONMENT

In a sword fight or other face-to-face combat, the environment would be the physical surroundings, the terrain, and the weather. In business, environment includes, to mention a few, market trends and structure, economic and political climate, technology, and public opinion. Resources and environment work together to provide the general setting in which a competitive situation arises and is resolved.

Musashi makes this comment about the purpose of careful analysis of the environment:

> *Determining an initial approach depends on your assessment of environment. Relative strength is a matter of fact. Approach derives from circumstances. Ask yourself this: Given the resources, environment, and attitudes involved in the competitive situation, is it better for me to adopt an offensive, defensive, or neutral approach to the conflict? No approach is better than another except in light of specific resource and environmental conditions.*

PRINCIPLE # 5: ATTITUDE

The attitude you bring to the conflict will be the attitude you have practiced in your training. You must be sharply aware of the reality of the moment. You must be confident and competent, aware and ready, neither afraid nor careless. Musashi teaches:

> *During competitive situations, your mind will be as you have conditioned it. In every moment, train yourself to be calm, expectant, observant. See things as they are. Do not be taken by surprise. Let your senses be open, your mind relaxed, your spirit balanced. Meet every challenge with a firm, yet flexible, attitude, centering your attention on determining reality.*

The essence of attitude is summed up in the code of the samurai warrior which underlies Musashi's feudal culture. The code instructs you to think only of winning in the situation you find yourself. If you fear the consequences of failure, you will begin to adjust your decisions and actions to take into account the possibility of failure. Failure must not be an option. Musashi says:

> *Even an otherwise useless person becomes valuable if he will not consider the possibility of failure and moves resolutely toward objectives.*

According to the samurai code, fear is the greatest enemy you face, far greater than any physical opponent. Your own fears magnify danger and obscure reality. But, fear exists only within your emotions and your perception. It does not have objective reality outside your mind. Whether you are afraid or not is a choice you make. And the choice you make does not change the facts of the situation.

Therefore, to win a battle, Musashi advises that you evaluate the situation and act with confidence. If you have practiced the REACT principles for executing tactics, you will be well prepared for whatever happens. Neither imagined fear nor false optimism, he says, can change your real position and circumstances. He adds:

If you face a tiger in the competitive jungle, it is in fact a tiger, neither something greater nor something less. You stand a far better chance with your eyes open and your spirit calm.

PRINCIPLE # 6: CONCENTRATION

In every situation, there are tactics which will work and tactics which will not work. According to Musashi:

Effective tactics are based on the principle of concentrating strength against weakness or resources into opportunity. Every opponent, every challenge you face, whether it is another human being, another company, or even change and innovation within your own company, has a weakness or opportunity you can exploit with the proper attention.

Concentration utilizes your resources most effectively against the weakness or opportunity contained in a specific situation or threat.

PRINCIPLE # 7: TIMING

After studying the history of competition in war, business, and politics, I have concluded that the timing of competitive actions is most often the critical factor in success.

Musashi constantly emphasizes the importance of timing and rhythm. Acting at the appropriate moment assures the best opportunity. He says:

> When you engage in competition, you should neither move too quickly nor too slowly. It is not speed in itself, but rhythm and timing, which are critical. The appropriate moment is that point in time when the scales are tipped in favor of the tactics you have chosen. Concentration and timing work together. If you do not concentrate both thought and resources at the appropriate moment, your tactics will probably fail.

These seven principles represent the core principles of Musashi's philosophy, the heart of his message, the hilt of the competitive sword. They are your framework for organizing the various themes which Musashi brings out in his text. Keep the principles in mind as you read the text. They are your ladder to understanding.

The true value of Musashi's principles is found in using them to win in competition. Business and military history are filled with examples of how successful executives and generals used Musashi's principles in order to succeed. In Part III of this book, Battle Tactics for Business, I discuss a number of master competitors who have succeeded by applying Musashi's concepts. In order to link tactics of master competitors clearly to Musashi's ideas, I will use the seven principles as guideposts. At this point, let's examine how Japanese auto companies employed these seven principles to succeed in penetrating the American car market.

JAPAN'S TACTICS FOR MARKET DOMINATION

The success of Japanese executives during the country's reconstruction period after World War II underscores my strong belief that understanding Musashi's tactical concepts provides a strong foundation for competitive success. Since Japan must import most of its raw materials, it could survive and prosper only by becoming a major and profitable exporter of manufactured goods and technology. Hence, building a globally competitive manufacturing base and improving manufacturing methods to world-class quality levels was a matter of life or death for Japanese companies.

Japanese business executives did not shrink from the task. When W. Edwards Deming, Shigeo Shingo, and others began teaching their highly effective methods for improving manufacturing operations and organization management through quantitative and statistical analysis, Japanese executives realized they had been handed a kind of "competitive sword" which they could wield successfully in world markets. American management was, at the time, ignoring the power of statistical analysis to improve design, production techniques, and quality for manufactured products. Applying Musashi's philosophy, Japanese executives perfected their ability to use this sword to beat their competition. And they are winning the battle.

Historically, there are three phases involved in most campaigns undertaken by Japanese industry. Each phase involves the application of ordered flexibility and critical attention to execution, resources, environment, attitude, concentration, and timing.

PHASE I: COPY TECHNOLOGY AND TRAIN PEOPLE

The principle of ordered flexibility strongly influences tactics in the first phase of the campaign. The Japanese initially enter a market in an organized manner, seeking information about industrial technology and customer attitude. They observe; they study; they experiment; they learn. This is the heart of ordered flexibility in business. Once reliable information has been obtained, they move in the most profitable direction. Musashi teaches:

> *Set up your organization so it approaches competitive challenges in an organized, disciplined manner (order), but is not limited in its choice of maneuvers (flexibility). The overall situation is easy to discern;*

the critical details are not. Hence, the competitive executive gathers together small pieces of information to create winning tactics. True and accurate assessment of circumstances is essential to winning. just like building a large statue from a small model. Practice day and night. Training is essential to success.

Japanese companies carefully consider factors related to execution (resources, environment, attitude, concentration, and timing) before and during a campaign. Musashi says:

The goal of your analysis of information is to provide focus. You cannot do everything, you cannot be everywhere. Proper focus allows you to allocate resources effectively to develop promising opportunities or to counter dangerous threats.

At the end of World War II, Japanese industrial production was actually in quite good shape. Although most of the cities had been destroyed by Allied bombing raids, the industrial base in the countryside was still very effective. The Japanese automobile and truck manufacturing industry was intact and operating. All it needed was raw materials and retooling to convert its production lines to manufacturing consumer, rather than military, vehicles. During this phase of the campaign, Japan was in a seriously weak resource position. Its main asset was its human capital, but it lacked most others, including important new technology that the US had developed during the war.

Japan could produce some goods; the problem, however, was selling them. Given the negative opinions of the Japanese in the US, the largest and most profitable market in the world was not immediately available. Time would blunt negative opinion, particularly if there was no additional provocation. The political environment of the world community would allow only passive and subtle maneuvers by the Japanese. The timing was wrong to push outwards on any front.

The attitude of the Japanese in response was one of patience and preparation. A great strength of the Japanese culture is the ability to copy and improve the creations of other countries. To use this strength, Japanese car companies quietly began buying American cars and disassembling them into their component parts (a process now called reverse engineering). This threatened no one at the time. Over a period of 10–15 years after the war, Japanese auto executives concentrated their actions on an organized program to learn how to build cars to American standards. They trained their engineers and assembly workers in the details of American automobile design and manufacturing by copying American cars. Armed with intimate knowledge of American automobile technology and the competitive sword of better manufacturing methods from Deming and others (at this point, American companies were not afraid to share technology with Japanese companies because they did not fear them as business competitors), the Japanese entered the next phase of tactics.

PHASE 2: RECOMBINE ELEMENTS AND WIDEN MARKET ACCEPTANCE

The second phase of the campaign involves concentration and timing. Musashi says:

After you have perfected your methods, you will gain a uniquely valuable freedom of action, a spontaneous ability to operate successfully even under most arduous conditions, an ability to overcome the most difficult challenges. Your reactions in competition should be natural and precise, governed by an intellect sharpened through daily practice. A skilled juggler can manage a large number of flying objects without concentrating on any one of them. He feels the rhythm in the movement of the objects as a whole. He adjusts his hands and feet in response to that rhythm without dropping anything. Constant practice allows him to concentrate without fixation.

Careful preparation allowed the Japanese to exploit the inattention of US car makers. Through concentration and timing, they were able to gain a toehold in the marketplace. The first Japanese automobile brand introduced into the American market was Toyota. The Japanese auto industry started with one car brand in order to minimize American reaction and maintain a low profile. A low profile would reduce the chances of a preemptive retaliatory strike by competitors in the US.

The Toyota vehicle built for the American market was small and plain. In the beginning, it was not taken seriously because it was underpowered compared to American cars. The general wisdom was that Japanese products were inferior. Toyota concentrated its efforts on experimenting with different products and options until it discovered combinations which began to gain acceptance in California and other West Coast markets.

When the time was right, other Japanese car manufacturers (Honda and Nissan) entered the US. Toyota had established a beachhead, now reinforcements were coming. Japanese autos began spreading across the country and taking significant market share from US companies. This is because the Japanese car had slowly, but firmly, established a reputation for being reliable, affordable transportation. The oil crisis of the 1970s also helped this process. With three major Japanese car companies successfully established in the United States, the stage was set to begin phase 3 of the tactics.

PHASE 3: INCREASE QUALITY/PRICE RATIO AND DOMINATE MARKET

In the third phase, which is still going on, Japanese auto makers have switched from defensive to offensive tactics. Offensive tactics succeed best when they focus strength on weakness and take advantage of opportunities presented by opponents. Musashi says:

Maintain unyielding determination. Constantly try to get the upper hand. Follow up every opportunity vigorously and thoroughly. Be relentless and constant. Allow the enemy no rest. The idea is to cause the competition to collapse. All things collapse when their time comes and their rhythm is destroyed. It is important to sense your opponent's rhythm. When his rhythm begins to deteriorate, he becomes vulnerable. If he recovers his rhythm, he can attack you again. In every conflict, there is an opportunity for you to win. A loss of momentum or poise in the opponent's stance will signal your chance. Be ready to strike at this moment.

You must focus all of your energy on striking the enemy at his moment of vulnerability. Make your attack direct and powerful. Cut the enemy down so that he is completely unable to recover or continue. Remember, when you fight, fight to win. Do not allow your enemy a chance to beat you by being careless, sloppy, or foolish.

Japanese car manufacturers are constantly increasing the quality/price ratio by offering innovative features and options on their vehicles. American cars either do not have these features and options, or they are available only on higher-priced models. The relative price for a Japanese car, given certain reliability levels and features, is lower than American cars. The Japanese make use of two obvious strengths: first, their products are generally better made than American products; and second, they keep weakening the Japanese yen with respect to the dollar in foreign exchange markets so the price of Japanese products is relatively lower. These strengths are aligned against exploitable American weaknesses.

Until Lexus (another Toyota product) was introduced, Japanese car models competed with mid-range American cars in price. Lexus opened up the luxury car market. It was quickly followed by Acura and Infinity. Market dominance is possible with this combination. The Japanese luxury car can be favorably compared to any lower-priced luxury car in the world, including Mercedes. It is certainly positioned to outclass American high-end vehicles, which can compete only on price.

This phase of tactics will continue into the future. American car makers are responding, with some success. At least they do not appear to be losing market share as quickly. But given the strength of the American dollar against the Japanese yen in 1998 due to the Asian economic crisis, the Japanese car is becoming cheaper than the American car for a given level of quality and features. I would expect Japanese car makers to push their advantage at this time. Indeed, the first quarter 1998 trade balance for the United States is $13 billion in the red, the largest negative trade balance in history. This is due primarily to the impact of apparent economic weakness in the Asian market.

Up until very recently, the Japanese auto industry effectively out-manufactured every other country in the world, on a per capita basis, in both quality and profitability. The discipline and structure of Musashi's approach to competition using the competitive sword of superior manufacturing quality and continuous process innovation, coupled with aggressive currency value management, gave Japan the strength and focus to rise from the ashes of defeat and become one of the world's greatest economies. It seems to me that it makes good sense to learn as much as possible about this approach and use it to your own advantage.

In Part III, I discuss a variety of examples of the applications of Musashi's principles to both modern business and military situations. Here are the examples I have chosen from modern business:

Howard Schultz (Starbucks)

The best example of the impact of competitive attitude in a large, successful business is Howard Schultz and Starbucks Coffee.

Warren Buffett

Buffett has made billions for himself and others by using creative, but fundamentally sound, analysis of resources and environment coupled with superb timing.

Andy Grove (Intel) and Bill Gates (Microsoft)

The stories of Andy Grove and Bill Gates show the immense power of sharply focused business thinking and concentrated tactics.

Donald Trump

"The Donald" is a master of timing and rhythm. In the real-estate business, timing is everything. Trump has built a fortune on doing the appropriate thing at the appropriate time in the appropriate rhythm.

Military history is another rich source of examples of how to apply Musashi's principles. I analyze four historical military situations in Part III. These situations will help you generalize, from another perspective, Musashi's principles for use in your own business and career.

The four situations are:

General Robert E. Lee and the Battles of Chancellorsville and Gettysburg

Lee's greatest success and (arguably) greatest failure are textbook examples of proper and improper use of ordered flexibility, focus, and execution.

General George Washington and the Battle of Trenton

Washington's analysis of the situation and execution were the keys to winning this pivotal battle in American history.

Lawrence of Arabia and Guerrilla Warfare in Arabia

Lawrence really understood the meaning of focus.

The Battle of Rorke's Drift in the Zulu War in Africa

This small, but ferocious, battle teaches the benefits of training, practice, and discipline coupled with sound assessment of the competitive situation and concentration of resources, particularly when one is caught in some very bad circumstances.

Some Words About the Text

Musashi wrote his material in a cave by the light of an oil lamp using crude pens, paper, and ink. It was composed over a period of several weeks or months. I suspect there have been a number of additions, rewrites, and reorganizations done by well-meaning scribes and students over the intervening centuries.

The writing is filled with admonitions about studying hard and practicing often. This is, of course, what one would expect when a teacher is writing to his disciples. As a result, the text is disorganized, tends to wander and repeat itself, and is generally unclear and confusing. The title of the original work is obscure in itself. The word "rings" means "aspects," "viewpoints," or "ways." The real subject of the book, sword fighting, is not explicitly mentioned in the title. If Musashi were writing this book for the popular business market today, the title would probably be something like Five Sure Ways to Win a Sword Fight Every Time Using Zen Philosophy, which is neither short nor memorable.

Musashi's writing style was greatly influenced by Zen philosophy. His writing, like many Zen masters, is deliberately vague. I think it was Confucius who said: "If a student cannot complete a figure after I have drawn the first stroke, he is not worth teaching." Zen masters seem to follow Confucius's instructional method. Hence, Zen writing tends to be indirect and obscure, laying the burden of understanding on the reader. This may be a good idea in teaching esoteric oriental philosophy, but it is not necessarily a practical one for learning competitive business methods.

In accordance with the original text, I have divided the material into five chapters (chapters are called "books" by Musashi); each chapter covers an identifiable business subject. Musashi named his five chapters — Earth, Water, Fire, Wind, and Void — after the five elements of nature. The original chapter titles were not closely related to the content and each chapter overlapped others to a greater or lesser degree.

Chapter titles used in this reinterpretation — Foundation, Form, Fire, Fabric, and Focus — are more representative of the content. I restructured the material somewhat to allow ideas to be developed logically, rather than simply asserted and repeated. In addition, where possible, I have substituted modern business language for medieval Japanese military terminology to make the application of ideas and methods clear.

Remember that the original text is not well grouped according to topic. Although there is some overall organization to the work, it tends to meander from point to point. Musashi often jumps from one subject to another and back again without transition. To counter his lack of consistency, I have inserted subheadings in each chapter to give you a general idea of what he intends to cover in a particular section. I cannot, however, eliminate the confusion entirely unless I arbitrarily reorder the whole text and subsequently destroy the originality and flavor of this literary classic. That is why you need to keep the seven principles in mind. If you do, the material will quickly make sense.

PART II
THE BOOK OF
FIVE RINGS FOR
EXECUTIVES

2

FOUNDATION

Becoming a master competitor and winning in competition should be the goals of a business executive's actions. This is the only path to power, profit, and prestige. Every successful executive must walk the path of competition for himself, on a personal level, and for his company, on an organizational level. No serious executive can afford to ignore this subject or treat it lightly.

OVERVIEW OF THE FIVE RINGS

In order to explain the principles of becoming a master competitor, I have divided this text into five "rings," that is, five aspects or topics. Each aspect has its own chapter. These five chapters are called Foundation, Form, Fire, Fabric, and Focus.

The Foundation chapter is an overview of my philosophy of competition, whether at a face-to-face level or at the organization-to-organization level. True understanding of the path of competition cannot be gained through mimicking the techniques of others. Techniques are superficial. You must learn to observe and assess a situation, comprehending both overall implications and critical details. Because a solid beginning leads to strong success, I call the first chapter Foundation.

The second chapter is called Form. The ideal competitive form follows the nature of water. When you think about the nature of water, think about both order and flexibility. Water is ordered in its objectives, but flexible in its approach. Water takes on the shape of the container which holds it, whether square or round. Water can be strong and powerful; water can be calm and pleasant. Water can be a drop or it can be an ocean. Water can be clear or it can be opaque. Water can kill or it can give life. Water can be heated to steam or frozen to ice; but, when left alone, it returns to its original liquid state. I model the ideal competitive form on the nature of water. I will call the form of water "ordered flexibility."

After you have mastered the principles of ordered flexibility, you will realize that the requirements of winning in a competitive situation are the same whether you face a single man or an entire industry. You can win every time because you understand the spirit of winning.

The competitive executive gathers together small pieces of information to create winning tactics. Just like building a large statue from a small model, he can understand ten thousand things from knowing just one simple process. It is difficult to write about this in detail. The principles of ordered flexibility are explained more fully in the Form chapter.

The third chapter is Fire. This chapter is specifically about competitive tactics in fights between individuals or small groups, such as face-to-face conflict or negotiating. The nature of fire is intense, whether the fire is small or large. It is the same thing with face-to-face competitive situations. The spirit of face-to-face competition is the same whether you are competing against just one person or striving against a team from a giant corporation. You must carefully understand the overall situation, while at the same time paying attention to the smallest detail.

The overall situation is easy to discern; the critical details are not. Think a moment about how soldiers move about during a skirmish. Once a large body of men begins to move in a certain direction, it takes time to change direction. So it is possible to predict where they are headed. One man, on the other hand, can change direction in an instant. His movements cannot be anticipated so easily.

Factors can change rapidly in the heat of competition. To keep up with this kind of rapid change, you must practice the principles of competition every day in your normal life. The steps in assessing situations and maintaining ordered flexibility should be as ordinary to you as breathing. Your spirit should remain unchanged, even under pressure. I write more about the nature of face-to-face competitive situations in the Fire chapter.

The fourth chapter is called Fabric. This chapter is more concerned with applying ordered flexibility to the challenges of managing people in organizations and meeting intense competition on a corporate level. Many philosophies and techniques of corporate management exist in the world. But all corporate management techniques are intended to support and facilitate corporate decisions and activities. The fabrics we wear are likewise intended to support and facilitate our lives. Adopting a certain fabric for your clothing determines how you will look, how warm or cool you will be, whether you get damp in the rain or whether you stay dry. You must understand the characteristics of fabrics before you can make a good choice. The characteristics of effective fabrics are simplicity, adaptability, durability. These same characteristics apply to choosing effective techniques for corporate management.

Simplicity facilitates understanding. Even if people practice a technique every day, if they do not understand the purpose of the technique and how to apply it under different competitive circumstances, they will not be able to use it when a difficult situation arises.

Adaptability fosters innovation. If people have mastered the details of a given technique through intense effort, but they do not understand the philosophy behind the technique and cannot adapt that philosophy to a specific situation, it will do little good in a crisis. Even a small misunderstanding can result in major errors in application.

Durability encourages profitability. Buying a new wardrobe each year requires great expenditures of time and money. The time and money spent to select and acquire clothing is taken away from other valuable activities. Changing management techniques frequently increases cost and diverts people's attention away from the main objective of business — generating wealth for business owners and employees.

It seems at times in the business world that executives under competitive stress are convinced that they can reduce managing competitive operations to some trick or technique and that this will provide an answer to their problems. Seeking a quick and simple solution is human nature, but it is the wrong approach. I have commented on aspects of selecting management techniques in the Fabric chapter so you can understand how to choose an effective technique for organizing people in challenging situations.

Fifth is the chapter on Focus. The ability to focus is your greatest asset in a competitive situation. When you appreciate the power of focus, you will feel the rhythm of your opponent and maintain control of his actions. You will understand his approach and effortlessly defeat him by naturally concentrating your attack in an appropriate place at an appropriate time.

You become a master competitor when you understand rhythm, timing, and control.

Extreme focus, however, creates dangerous weakness. If you allow it, your opponent can exploit your focus by emphasizing the competitive details which favor his objectives. In this way he tries to manipulate your perceptions and lead you where he wants you to go. Attaining the way of the master competitor means seeing the implications of details, but not allowing them to control you; it means understanding the nature of a situation and the rhythm of competitive activities. It means operating at a level beyond conscious thought. I will show you this in the Focus chapter.

COMPETITIVE BASICS

People can choose from several possible directions in life. Ministers, priests, and rabbis help people achieve personal salvation. Scholars and scientists seek answers to the riddles of the universe. Poets and artists raise the level of culture. Physicians save lives. Each person selects a direction according to personal taste and talent. Ambitious executives should have a taste for competition and the desire to learn the art of competitive success.

Walking the path of competition requires a balance of technical competence and individual confidence. Even if an executive lacks natural ability in one of these areas, he should do his best to constantly improve himself.

As a rule, even ordinary people understand that executives must readily accept the consequences which arise from success or failure, winning or losing, in competitive situations. But people from all walks of life also face the consequences of success and failure every day, whether they are prepared for it or not. The difference between a serious executive and an ordinary person is that the serious executive purposefully studies how to use men, materials, and money to gain power, profit, and prestige. Success is not left to the winds of fate nor the whims of others. This is the real benefit of learning the path of competition.

Even though most people face situations in which their actions can cause gain or loss, there are still some who believe that studying the path of competition will not benefit them. When one looks at life realistically, however, one can see that competition on a personal and organizational level is present in most human situations. This is particularly true in business, where people are always trying to gain an advantage. The path of competition is truly useful because its lessons can be applied at all times in all things.

Over the entire world, masters of the path of competition win fame and fortune. All executives must study these principles if they wish to excel. The field of management, however, is filled with showmen, charlatans, and pirates. These people are concerned only with quick profit and apparent gains. They care nothing for true wisdom or excellence. Employing their methods is a major cause of loss and confusion.

These phony prophets make a living by teaching buzzword management. They call themselves "wizards of competition," but in reality they preach only the latest fad or fantasy. In recent times especially, one siren song after another has gained popularity. "Buzzword management" always looks attractive and sounds easy; its proponents are smooth and slick on the surface. Those fronting the latest fad would have you think that their ideas were transmitted from the gods. But, if you scratch the surface, the ideas soon dissipate.

If you observe the world of business today, you can see executives trying in vain to use these popular techniques for managing groups and organizations. Unpracticed executives sometimes believe that techniques alone can substitute for wisdom and training. But techniques tend to ignore people. People are often viewed as commodities to be exploited and discarded. Under this way of thinking, impressions are more valuable than substance. People become disposable plastic implements, molded for a specific purpose, used up, and then disposed of when they are no longer needed.

True success in competitive situations does not depend on the fad or technique being used. Since ancient times, it has been known that it is the discipline and skill of the individual using the technique which determine success or failure. It goes without saying that people who are purveyors of buzzwords alone cannot prevail against people who are practiced masters of the art of competition.

EXECUTIVE FUNCTIONS

In operating businesses, executives perform different functions. For instance, they can work in marketing, in finance, in operations. But, whatever the specific area, a serious executive must train his thinking to a broader and deeper than level that of a mere functional technician.

In the marketing function, practitioners use various statistics to determine market parameters. They may spend years cultivating a new product so it will be profitable. Marketers pay attention to people's tastes and behaviors. They must aggressively seek new ways to serve their customers. This is the way of marketing.

In the finance function, workers control the uses of funds and track the inflows and outflows of capital. Workers in this function must be precise in their thinking and conservative in their outlook. This is the way of finance.

In operations, people make goods and deliver services. They must efficiently apply technology to create their products at the lowest possible cost within a given range of quality. Operations people are orderly; they must pay attention to details of designs, schedules, and materials. They must time their actions properly. This is the way of operations.

THE MASTER ORGANIZER

In organizing the various functional areas to work smoothly in a business, a serious executive uses the same methods that a master carpenter uses in constructing a building. If you want to learn the art of building a competitive organization, read this material carefully and think about it deeply. The teacher is the needle, while the student is the thread.

A master carpenter must practice his trade in order to compete. It is essential for the carpenter to continuously improve his level of skill. He maintains the sharpness of his tools and has them ready to use at all times. He follows the directions of his employer; his measurements are precise; his actions are efficient; his results are superior.

The goal is to fashion beautiful and useful objects, to become recognized as a consummate craftsman. When the carpenter assembles a cabinet, it must not be warped; the joints must be correctly aligned; the surfaces must be sanded smooth; the finish must be deep and even; there must be no obvious defects.

The master carpenter is an expert in the use of tools, materials, and people. He must be able to develop precise plans based on the overall requirements of his employer. He must measure dimensions accurately and perform his job according to the plan. The master carpenter earns his living by assuring that each job is completed on time and within budget.

The master carpenter understands how different types of structures are constructed. He studies plans and purposes to decide what kinds of subcontractors he needs to employ in order to create the desired result. Because the master carpenter is the chief supervisor of the subcontractors working on a project, it is also his responsibility to know the building codes and regulations for the locality where the structure is being built. He must know the desires, attitudes, and peculiarities of his client. He must follow the rules of his own profession.

Before starting construction, the master carpenter sorts the lumber. When building a house, for instance, he uses strong, straight, and attractive pieces of wood, without knots, for the entry columns. He uses straight pieces with only small defects for less obvious columns. He uses wood that is not quite as strong, but is beautiful to look at, for stairs, door frames, and window sills. He carefully uses wood that is strong, but contains visible defects, within the structure to provide long-lasting strength without detracting from overall appearance. He even uses wood that is weak and defective for scaffolding to help during construction. Later he cuts up the scaffolding for firewood.

The master carpenter watches his workers carefully, leaving nothing to chance. To assure continuous progress towards his goal, he makes it his business to know the limitations of each individual. He does not assign work that is either too easy or too hard. Thus, he walks among his workers and talks to them. He watches morale and attitudes closely. When someone needs encouragement, he provides it. He is quick to praise achievement, but just as quick to correct weakness.

The master carpenter assigns jobs to people based on their level of skill. Those who work can work quickly and carefully are given greater, more independent, responsibility. Those who lack ability, training, or desire are assigned less important work and are supervised closely. If the master carpenter puts the right person in the right job, the work will continue without mistakes or interruption until it is completed.

To learn the way of the master organizer, study the methods of the master carpenter. Practice them in your life at all times.

PERSONAL POWER

On a personal level, the power used by executives in competitive operations is generated from two main sources: power can be derived from competence (i.e., technical skill, education, experience, and management talent) and from confidence (i.e., interpersonal skills, personality, character, and spirit). These sources of personal power must be used in balance. An overemphasis on either competence or confidence can result in defeat. Great strength and great weakness are two faces of the same coin. The advantage goes to those who use competence and confidence together.

Competence and confidence are complementary aspects of executive power. When one understands the situation, one can use the appropriate tool according to the specific time, place, and circumstances.

An executive may possess attributes such as an imposing presence, important connections, or impressive surroundings, but these attributes are not essential. They can be used as tools by those with skill. But they will not, in themselves, win a battle if either competence or confidence is lacking.

Serious executives who want to master the art of competition should practice with the understanding that both competence and confidence are required. When you are in a fight, it is unwise to leave some of your weapons unused. It is stupid to lose if you have not tried everything. When a person has overly developed either his competence or his confidence, he will find it difficult to win in a situation which is unsuited to his strength. Hence, I strongly advocate a balanced approach in order to ensure you have the best chance in all types of situations.

Confidence is best used in situations where you have close contact with other people in direct supervision, face-to-face competition, or negotiation. Competence, on the other hand, can be used in situations where there is an organizational or geographical distance between parties. A reputation for great competence inspires awe in our associates and our competitors. When combined with appropriate confidence, competence is difficult to overcome even at a distance. But, between two executives of equal competence, the one with greater confidence will win.

Being overly competent, but lacking in confidence and other people skills, is like trying to fight with a long, heavy sword held in both hands. This tactic works well if you are standing still on level ground, facing your enemy, and your enemy is willing to attack you from the front. But a long, heavy sword is awkward if you must fight on horseback, if you must run away down a rocky or uneven path, if you must wade through a swamp, or if you face a group of people who are coming at you from several different directions.

When you are fighting many battles or competitors at once, it is a better tactic to have several weapons. To be effective in difficult competitive situations, you must be able to use whatever power is needed, when it is needed. You cannot be completely dependent on one approach, but rather must be able to appropriately meld together the strengths of many approaches. If you try to defeat your enemies with competence alone, you will fail as often as you succeed. If you try to defeat your enemies with confidence alone, they will eventually expose your weakness.

When you can defeat an enemy with only one approach, do so. It should not be that difficult, in normal situations, if you have experience and expertise. But you should always practice using both competence and confidence together in order to balance your attack and defense.

Different or unusual situations may require emphasis on one competitive aspect or another. In managing groups and organizations, the power of competence is emphasized because competence can be effectively transferred through organizational levels. In face-to-face competition and negotiation, the power of confidence can be more important. But, no matter what type of competition is involved, competence and confidence are powers which are complementary and reinforce one another.

The specific competitive situation determines which aspects and tactics will be more effective. Precise approaches and combinations cannot be stipulated in advance. The way of the master competitor is to win no matter what the circumstances by understanding the situation and using an appropriate approach at an appropriate time.

When we have developed our strength in one area we tend to rely on that strength. Acquiring and using other strengths can be difficult at first. All things, at first, are uncomfortable and difficult to use. When you become used to both competence and confidence, you will gain the power of the master competitor. Many of these ideas cannot be explained in detail. Learn the principles; they can be applied in ten thousand situations.

The proper use of executive power cannot be learned in a classroom. Classroom training is often overly concerned with fine details which, in practice, are not important. One must be able to adapt the principles of competition to diverse circumstances under great stress. If you become narrowly focused in your approach, you will have difficulty in evolving your techniques to meet changing conditions.

When you have attained mastery of competence and confidence, you will have the power to defeat ten others by yourself. If it is possible for one person to defeat ten, then it is possible for ten to defeat one hundred, or for one thousand to defeat ten thousand. Whether you face one opponent or ten thousand, the principles are the same.

STANDARD APPROACHES

Beware of dependence on standard approaches in competitive situations. Standard approaches are predictable. In every standard approach, there is a weakness which can be exploited by the competition.

If you become predictable, you will be defeated. The unexpected cannot be predicted. Innovative improvisation based on sound principles leads to victory.

Too much emphasis on impressions and not enough emphasis on substance makes one vulnerable in critical situations.

No particular tactic is preferable to another all the time. It is the circumstances which determine which approach will succeed. Do not become rigid; if you do, you will break once the battle starts.

Observe the impact of your actions. Watch your competitor's reactions. This is essential to success. It is not enough to execute an action. You must also track the effect of that action. One virtue of using a bow in combat is that you can follow the flight of an arrow and make adjustments to your aim.

To take full advantage of the path of competition, you must also learn something about other paths. Priests, musicians, teachers, and artisans follow different paths. Nevertheless, a basic knowledge of many activities will help you apply your path to a wide range of situations. Learning other ways will add polish and variety to your tactics.

USING PEOPLE

The people you depend on to execute your tactics should have good stamina and even temperaments. As a rule, dedicated and hard-working associates are best.

In general, to win a battle, your close associates should be strong and capable. They should stand up well to intense pressure. People should be chosen for dependability rather than decoration.

In using people, as in using tools, one should not choose the same person every time. Use the most appropriate person for the task. This means you must become familiar with the strengths and habits of your entire cadre. It is bad for executives to play favorites in competitive situations. Becoming too dependent on certain individuals fosters weakness. Learn to be objective and practical.

TIMING

When you engage in competition, you should neither move too quickly nor too slowly. It is not speed in itself but rhythm and timing which are critical.

All tactical success is based on correctly understanding rhythm and timing. This is particularly true in competition. In every contest, there are moments which favor victory. Practice so you can understand these moments.

Musicians and dancers depend on timing. Performances are enjoyable only if players are in rhythm. Rhythm is also present in competitive activities, although it is not as obvious. If you can discern the rhythm of your competitor's actions, you can always defeat him. During an executive's career, there are rhythms of advancement and rhythms of decline; rhythms of prosperity and rhythms of scarcity; rhythms of success and rhythms of failure.

Timing is particularly important when deciding when to move and when to stand still. The timing of the rhythms determines whether we grow wealthy or become impoverished. Rising and falling rhythms occur in every activity. Your success depends on your ability to tell the difference.

There are many other rhythms in competitive situations. You must understand all the rhythms present — the great ones, the small ones, the slow ones, the fast ones, the ones in the forefront, and the ones in the background. Understand which rhythms can overturn your plans and which can be used to overturn your competition. You will not become a master competitor unless you can read your opponent's rhythm and understand how to disrupt it without becoming confused yourself.

Success in competition comes from sensing your competitor's timing and striking him in a rhythm that he does not expect. You must manage advances and retreats with precise timing. All five chapters in this book concern themselves with timing. Train yourself to recognize it and to use it.

Rules for Master Competitors

For those who wish to become master competitors, here is a summary of the rules of conduct which will make it easier:

1. Do what is right. Study what is correct.
2. Sense the rhythm and timing in everyday situations.
3. Broaden your knowledge of the practice of management.
4. Study other arts and professions.
5. Distinguish between profitable and unprofitable matters.
6. See reality under all circumstances.
7. Look for that which is not obvious.
8. Concentrate on critical details.
9. Eliminate useless activity.

If you work every day with these rules in mind, you will eventually learn how to win in competition. Look at things broadly so you can adapt the rules to many situations. An executive who attains complete understanding will not lose even against great odds.

Most importantly, devote yourself to winning by using the way of the master competitor. Very soon, you will be able to beat most opponents on an individual level since you will have trained your mind to see how to win at any time. If you develop your skill, you will have a powerful psychological advantage, no matter where you are. If you always have the advantage, how can any person defeat you?

On a larger scale, the serious executive will win by keeping good employees with him, organizing activities well, bearing himself correctly, increasing profits, and generating wealth. The key to managing people is developing competence and confidence, creating within yourself a competitive spirit which will not allow defeat. This will strengthen you in adversity and bring you ultimate success. This is the way of the master competitor.

3

FORM

ORDERED FLEXIBILITY

The essence of my method of tactical thinking is based on the nature of water which is, at the same time, both ordered and flexible. I call this chapter "Form" because your competitive form and structure must be based on ordered flexibility, so you can adapt your methods to different situations to achieve your goals.

The ideal of ordered flexibility is summed up in the concept of "positioning without position." As soon as your opponent recognizes your tactical approach, he can defeat it. Therefore, excessive order and structure lead to brittleness and defeat. On the other hand, if you have no order whatsoever, you cannot concentrate your resources nor time your actions effectively. This also leads to defeat. Balance order with flexibility.

Flow like water around obstacles. Move carefully when conditions are unfavorable; move powerfully when the right course opens up. Everyone knows that water in a stream seeks the sea (water is ordered in its objectives), but who can tell how it will get there (water is flexible in its approach)? Think of winning, not of position.

Ordered flexibility is the key to winning. Content yourself with reality. Seek it, understand it, mold your actions to it. Achieve what you must in response to your opponent. Wait for your opportunities. They will surely come. But make no mistakes yourself because your opponent is watching you.

A casual reading of my explanation of competitive thinking will not allow you to apply it when you are in the midst of a crisis. Every word must be carefully considered beforehand. Superficial understanding will lead to costly errors.

To illustrate the principles of competitive success, I use examples of combat between individuals and groups. This is not because I value combat for itself. Combat is costly, destructive, and dangerous. Anything can happen in combat. Most things that do happen are undesirable and expensive. View the examples broadly so that you can attain understanding at a level which allows you to apply the principles quickly and correctly in your specific situation. Combat is a convenient metaphor. Use these ideas to win without fighting if you can.

Competitive situations are different from other aspects of life. There are important issues at stake in competitive situations. The rewards and penalties are serious. If you intend to succeed in competitive situations, you cannot afford to become even a little bit confused or bewildered. If you misapply these principles only slightly, you will be defeated.

Mastering the art of competition is not just a matter of reading these words. One cannot learn the secrets of winning tactics in an afternoon. These principles must be absorbed so thoroughly that they come forth automatically. The true path of victory is more accurately recognized at an instinctive level; the best application of these ideas comes from within you and is shaped in the moment of need. Competitive genius grows in the spirit, but the seed is planted through unremitting study. Prepare constantly.

During competitive situations, your mind will be as you have conditioned it. In every moment, train yourself to be calm, expectant, observant. See things as they are. Do not be taken by surprise. Let your senses be open, your mind relaxed, your spirit balanced. Meet every challenge with a firm, yet flexible, attitude, centering your attention on determining reality.

When your body is relaxed, keep your mind alert. When your body is hurried, keep your mind calm. Do not allow your mind to control your body, nor your body to control your mind. In this way, you will act appropriately. Do not allow others to read your thoughts. Pay attention to reality; do not let your judgment be subverted by emotion. If you are weak in a certain situation, you must be able to think as if you were strong; if you are strong, you must be able to think as if you were weak. See things from your opponent's point of view. True and accurate assessment of circumstances is essential to winning.

Let your spirit be fluid, flexible, and free. Look at things broadly. Grow in wisdom and education. Sharpen your mind. When you can distinguish between what is right and what is wrong, what is real and what is false, what is substance and what is illusion, you will have the competence to compete. When you are unmoved by the threat of loss or the promise of gain, you will attain the confidence to win.

STEADINESS

There is a special strength in mastering the art of competition, particularly face-to-face negotiation or conflict. Even in the heat of battle, you will remain calm. Nothing upsets your competitors and inspires your companions like steadiness under pressure.

In face-to-face negotiation or conflict, physical bearing is important. Hold yourself erect. Keep your face composed. Do not wrinkle or distort your features. Do not register emotion with your eyes. Do not unintentionally make distracting motions or noises. This is a sign of nervousness.

As with the mind, your natural bearing should not change in competitive situations. Your combat bearing and your ordinary bearing should be the same. Think carefully about why this is so.

An important aspect of winning in competition is knowing your opponent's capabilities. Do not be deceived or unbalanced by obvious distractions or misleading actions. This takes discipline and confidence.

See and understand the activity around you. Look into the heart of the matter. Sort out significant movements from insignificant movements. Perceive everything, not just those things your opponent intends for you to perceive. The ability to understand events that are far away by observing events that are close and the ability to keep events that are close from overwhelming your judgment are the roots of competitive success.

PERSPECTIVE

It is necessary to think things through before entering competition. You should consider both the large view and the narrow view. The rules of winning are the same whether the battle is between two people or two armies.

Keep your perspective. Do not look at one thing and forget about another. Maintaining perspective and confidence under pressure are skills that are learned over time.

In using my method of thinking in competitive situations, you must apply the principles naturally. If you are overly tense, you will make mistakes. If you are inattentive or careless, you will miss important details. Be aware and ready, neither too tense nor too loose, neither too ordered nor too flexible. The concept of ordered flexibility is designed to help you respond quickly and effectively. If you use the concept properly, you will not fail to consider all relevant issues, both for yourself and for your opponent. What could be more useful for a person who is serious about winning?

Recognize the significance of what is written here. Practice using the techniques of success in every situation, every day. Do not deviate from the truth under any circumstances. The way you train is the way you perform. Train hard.

Execution and Competitive Analysis (REACT)

Execution is the action you take to achieve your objectives. Excellent execution is critical to success. Excellent execution consists of two equally important elements: first, appropriate tactics; second, appropriate timing. In other words, to win in competition, you must take an appropriate action at an appropriate time. You must not, and cannot, insist on perfection in your actions. Perfection takes too long. And who can control every variable in a situation? Even an imperfect stroke will destroy an enemy who is unprepared for it.

Analysis based on the REACT principles (resources, environment, attitude, concentration, timing) will help you assess and deal with specific situations and accomplish your objectives through appropriate operational tactics. Use REACT to determine appropriate actions and appropriate times.

When you are engaged in competition, evaluate the following. First, resources: resources are those assets and skills which each side brings to the conflict. Resources are the raw material of tactics. In business, resources can include people, plant and equipment, finances, and reputation. In all competitive situations, however, the most critical resource is timely and accurate information.

Second, environment. In a sword fight or face-to-face confrontation, the environment would be the physical surroundings, the terrain, and the weather. In business, environment includes market trends and structure, economic and political climate, technology, and public opinion. Resources and environment work together to provide the general setting in which a competitive situation arises and is resolved.

Third, control your attitude. The attitude you bring to the conflict is the attitude you have practiced in your training. You must focus on the reality of the moment. You must be confident and competent, aware and ready, neither afraid nor careless.

The essence of attitude is summed up in the code of the samurai warrior. Think only of winning in the situation you find yourself. If you either fear failure or anticipate success, you will begin to adjust your decisions and actions to take the expected outcome into account. Neither the consequences of failure nor the benefits of success must be considered during the fight. Even an otherwise useless person becomes valuable if he will not consider either failure or success and moves resolutely toward objectives.

Fear is the greatest enemy you face, far greater than any physical opponent. Your own fears magnify danger and obscure reality. But fear exists only within yourself. It does not have reality outside your mind. Whether you are afraid or not is a choice you make. And the choice you make does not change the facts of the situation.

The belief that success is certain, on the other hand, makes one careless. If you cannot lose, why take the time to carefully evaluate the situation? If I were your enemy, this is exactly the way I would want you to feel.

Therefore, evaluate the situation carefully and then act with confidence. If you have lived and practiced my method of competitive thinking, you will be well prepared. Neither imagined fear nor false optimism can change your real position and circumstances. If you face a tiger, it is in fact a tiger, neither something greater nor something less. You stand a far better chance with your eyes open and your spirit calm.

Fourth, concentration. Concentrate resources to create advantage. In order to concentrate your resources effectively, you must be aware of everything, the larger picture and the smaller details. In every situation, there are tactics which work and tactics which do not work. Winning tactics are based on the principle of concentrating strength against weakness. Every opponent, every challenge you face, whether it is another human being or another company, has a weakness you can exploit. In every battle, there is an approach which can win. Concentration utilizes your resources best against a specific threat or challenge.

And fifth, timing. Time your movements. After studying the history of competition in war, business, and politics, I have noted that the timing of competitive actions is most often the critical factor in success. Acting at the appropriate moment ensures the best opportunity to win. The appropriate moment is that point when the scales are tipped in favor of the tactics you have chosen. Concentration and timing work together. If you do not concentrate both thought and resources at the appropriate moment with the best people in charge, your tactics will probably fail.

POSITION

Be on guard at the beginning of the competition. Assess your position with respect to your competitor's position along two dimensions: relative strength and initial posture. In terms of relative strength, you are either stronger than your opponent, weaker than your opponent, or your strengths are balanced. In terms of initial posture, you may take an offensive stance, a defensive stance, or you may be neutral. Assessing strength and posture provides a basis for selecting tactics.

Whether you adopt an offensive, defensive, or neutral initial posture depends on the situation. Choose your posture according to what is advantageous in the circumstances.

Determining an initial posture depends on your assessment of resources, environment, and attitude. Relative strength is always a matter of fact at a given moment. Posture, though, derives from circumstances. Ask yourself this: Given the resources, environment, and attitudes involved in the immediate competitive situation, is it better for me to adopt an offensive, defensive, or neutral posture? No posture is better than another except in the light of specific conditions.

No matter what your beginning position, your only objective should be winning. If your goal is to tie, or not to be defeated, you will eventually lose. Think only of how to win.

Maintaining Balance

The essence of success in competition is understanding balance. As long as your strength and posture are balanced relative to your opponent, given the environment of the competition, you can compete effectively. For instance, if you are weaker in resources, you can balance with superior attitude, speed, timing, and clever tactics. This was the secret of General Robert E. Lee's success in the American Civil War. (For more discussion of General Lee, see Battle Tactics for Business, Part III.) Remember, no matter whether you are stronger or weaker than your opponent, you can always win if you are confident and competent, and you control the time and place of the competition. You must take this to heart.

Knowing the path of competition requires complete mastery of these principles. Using ordered flexibility must be as natural as breathing.

DELIBERATE SPEED

When faced with a crisis, if you try to act quickly when you are not adequately prepared, it will be hard to avoid mistakes. Facing a crisis successfully means acting calmly and moving deliberately at an appropriate speed.

Moving too quickly throws you off balance, thereby reducing your ability to respond effectively. You can win most often when you move at the right speed, neither too fast nor too slow.

When you respond to a challenge, it is essential that you do an appropriate thing at an appropriate time. Doing the first thing that comes to mind, doing what you did last year, or doing what your opponent wants you to do only leads to difficulty. When you have learned ordered flexibility, you will meet challenges with your eyes and your mind open to reality and possibility. Work at this.

REALITY AND INFORMATION

Ordered flexibility guides your selection of operational tactics. It matters less which initial posture you choose than how well you are able to use the moves of your opponent to your own advantage. You must win in the situation you find yourself.

To remain flexible, know the enemy's capabilities, plans, and rhythms before the battle. Devise strategies to defeat the enemy's plans so you can win without combat if possible. Understanding the enemy is key to success.

Gather information from every possible source. Leave no stone unturned. Use spies, consultants, informants. Perceiving the enemy's strategy allows you to defeat it. Knowing the enemy's position and movement prevents unpleasant surprises.

Information is the fabric of tactics. You can never know too much about your enemy, yourself, or the situation.

The goal of your analysis of information is to provide focus. You cannot do everything, you cannot be everywhere. Proper focus allows you to allocate resources effectively to develop promising opportunities or to counter dangerous threats.

Every tactic, approach, or idea you have has both advantages and disadvantages. Any appropriate set of tactics can win; all tactics can lose. It is only with respect to specific situations that tactics succeed or fail. Every conflict contains opportunities to win and to lose. Respect your opponent. Understand his methods. This is the path of victory.

PERFORMANCE AND TRUST

Executing tactics based on ordered flexibility also depends on the ability and willingness of people to perform in critical situations. Executives must trust, and be trusted by, their subordinates and associates. Only with trust can people be counted on to exert maximum effort during a crisis.

Give incentives to those employees who are ambitious and competent. Instruct those who are ignorant. Remove those who repeatedly fail. In this way, ambitious, competent employees will be motivated to succeed; lazy, careless employees will fear failure.

Trust is developed through training and practice. Employees who are well trained, strictly but fairly disciplined, and treated with respect will perform well in a crisis.

SITUATIONS AND TACTICS

Different situations give rise to different responses. Consider the following points carefully. To understand the essence of ordered flexibility, think a moment about engaging an opponent in a fight. Which initial position do you adopt? What choices do you have? Is there any advantage to a given initial position? For instance, whether you are in fact weaker or stronger than your opponent, is there any advantage to appearing either weaker or stronger at the outset? Is it better to be aggressive or passive? The answers to these questions lie in knowledge of your opponent and his motivations.

In the absence of specific knowledge, the best position to take at the outset of a competition is the middle position, neither weaker nor stronger, neither passive nor aggressive. If you have an advantage in a fight, position your resources where the advantage can benefit you. An intelligent enemy (and who can afford to assume the enemy is stupid?) will be aware of his own weaknesses and will try to maneuver you into a position where your advantage is minimized.

If you are at a disadvantage, narrow the field of competition. Find weak spots in the enemy's front and concentrate strength on weakness. Do the unexpected. Keep the enemy off balance.

Fighting a battle on familiar territory gives one a defensive advantage. But it is only by taking the battle to the enemy that one can win. Taking the battle to the enemy is a matter of information and timing.

Deceiving the enemy is essential to winning. If the enemy knows your strength and your plans, even if you are stronger, he can defeat you. Therefore, if you know you are strong, appear weak. Then move swiftly when the enemy exposes his own weakness.

In face-to-face confrontation, an arrogant enemy is a careless enemy. Observe carefully. Speak softly. Make obvious, intentional mistakes. Bumble a little. If your opponent underestimates you, you have a great opportunity to win. Confuse the enemy with unpredictable movement and sudden noise. Appear distracted. Watch your enemy's response. This will expose his thoughts and his weaknesses.

Create strategic alliances to gain strength. Develop mutually beneficial relationships with valuable allies. Make sure those who are important to your success benefit from it.

Be prepared to act when the opportunity arises. This requires both courage and patience, order and flexibility. The ability to perceive and benefit from the moment of advantage is developed through constant study and practice.

You are particularly vulnerable when you are changing your position. Be prepared for ambush.

If possible, destroy your opponent's sources of capital and people. Without money and talent, he is helpless.

If you are moving into unfamiliar territory, be sure you employ local guides and consultants. Study the battleground carefully. Make the enemy come to you. A strong position, combined with good timing, guarantees success.

Do not attack an enemy who has a strong defensive position. Wait for an opportunity. Better to delay an attack than to fail. If you cannot win, wait. Defend yourself carefully. Conserve your strength.

When you are facing a clever enemy and cannot put yourself in a position where you have a clear advantage, pull back and wait for a better time. Surprise is your most effective weapon against a well-managed opponent.

Attack a disordered enemy quickly, providing your troops are trained and disciplined. But do not pursue a retreating enemy too vigorously. You may be caught in a trap.

A well-ordered enemy formation should be watched, but not challenged. Be alert and ready. First weaken their morale and wear down their diligence. When they are tired and discouraged, then attack.

At times, direct attack cannot be avoided. Engage in a direct attack with well-trained, well-rested, and well-supplied soldiers. A direct attack on an opponent of equal strength can only succeed through deception and improvisation. Fooling the enemy is generally more profitable than directly attacking him.

Keep your head in a crisis. When emotions are running high, reality can become distorted. If you are calm and observant, you will see how to win. Practice facing a crisis each day in your mind. Thus, when the crisis finally arrives, you will act as you do on any other day. This will inspire your followers to be stable and have courage. Those who are prepared to be steady under pressure will survive in difficult situations.

Lure your opponent into carelessness with the promise of easy gains. Greed destroys perception. Do not let it destroy your own! Do not allow yourself to be provoked or coerced into rashness. When the enemy reveals an apparent advantage, before rushing in headlong, make sure you understand the enemy's strategy and his strength. If the advantage is real, seize it. But remember, most of the time the enemy will cover his weaknesses carefully. Watch for deceptions and traps.

Fight the enemy when he is short on supplies and manpower. If the enemy is confused, attack quickly.

Control the time and place of battle. Force the enemy to come to you. Do not put yourself in a position where the enemy can choose the time and place of battle. Retain the initiative.

Enemies become more dangerous after they have been defeated in a battle. Losers want to be winners. They will attack again if given the opportunity. Be alert.

On the other hand, when you have been defeated, do not lose heart. Salvage what you can, regroup and watch for your chance. The enemy may relax if he thinks you are not dangerous.

Take your time to make sure preparations for battle are thorough and complete. But when it comes time to fight, seek a quick victory. Anything can happen in a fight. The longer you are exposed to the risks of combat, the greater your chances for defeat from unforeseen elements. Battlefield conditions change rapidly. Maintain flexibility in attitude and in formation.

Appropriate concentration and dispersion of resources are essential to success. Focus strength on weakness; faster on slower; greater on lesser. If you can win, concentrate your forces and gain victory; if you cannot win, disperse your forces and avoid defeat.

High morale is critical to success in difficult situations. Give your troops good reasons for believing in themselves. Give your troops valuable rewards if they succeed.

If you attack something the enemy considers necessary, he must defend himself. If you defend something the enemy cannot attack, you are not in danger.

Leave your enemy an avenue of escape. When he becomes discouraged or frightened, he will run away. Be especially careful when an enemy who is under pressure begins to negotiate. He is trying to gain time.

When you are facing an opponent in serious conflict, think always of stabbing him in the eye, his point of greatest vulnerability. When you strike at the opponent's eye, he will try to protect himself and become vulnerable in other areas. In the midst of a battle, as soon as your opponent tries to defend himself or to get out of the way, you can find a way to win.

THE ESSENCE OF VICTORY

In order to obtain victory over others in competition, you must first learn to apply ordered flexibility completely. Understand the spirit of competing and the skills necessary to win. Then, you and your group will act with one coordinated mind, able to naturally comprehend which tactics are best for the situation you are in. This is the way you achieve victory over others. You cannot learn how to win by just reading a book. You must practice constantly. You must always think of how to respond to challenges. The ordered flexibility method of thinking described in this book give you the means to succeed in all competitive situations.

You can win every time if you see the essence of the situation. Hone your ability to discern the motives and tactics of others at a glance. Do not wait for a crisis before learning how to apply ordered flexibility. If you train diligently, success will come from the heart. You will not have to decide how to respond to a threat; you will already know. There is a time in every conflict when victory can be won. Ordered flexibility will allow you to seize the moment.

Walk down the path towards mastery of competition with patience, one step at a time, keeping the principles of victory in your mind and heart.

The master competitor wins over himself first. Do not allow your attention to wander. Be consistent and steady in your approach. You can gain intuitive understanding of situations if you challenge yourself in practice.

Once you master yourself, you can master others. Pay attention to the details presented in this book and you will eventually be able to master all those around you.

4

FIRE

In organization-to-organization or face-to-face conflict, competitive tactics can be viewed like fire. Fire can be a friend or an enemy, an offensive force or a defensive shield. Competitive tactics likewise can bring victory or cause defeat. Fire must be handled with care. Competitive tactics must be executed effectively. The nature of fire is an intense combination of elements. Competitive situations are the same. This Fire chapter discusses the elements of victory and defeat in conflict.

Some people think about competitive tactics in a narrow sense. They try to win battles by concentrating on learning insignificant or clever maneuvers. These people can be compared to someone who is accustomed to killing flies with a fly swatter. Against a fly, you may gain victory by flicking your weapon a little faster. In truth, you can probably kill more flies by practicing deft movements of your wrist and training yourself in trifles. But, against a tiger in the jungle, a fly swatter is useless, no matter how refined and perfected your movements.

Looking at the history of competition through the ages, in situation after situation where lives and fortunes have been at stake, the winners were masters of the art of competition. They used ordered flexibility to determine the strengths and weaknesses of their opponents and to assess their own position. They understand which weapons are appropriate and how to wield those weapons effectively. When one is looking into the eyes of a tiger, one should not think of swatting flies.

Ordered flexibility is the only way to guarantee victory when you are fighting for your life. The principles of winning a contest are the same whether you are talking about one person against ten opponents or one thousand against ten thousand. Consider this carefully.

Of course, in business, it is generally impossible to assemble one thousand, one hundred, or even ten competent opponents to practice against. But you can master ordered flexibility by constantly training yourself in every situation you experience. If you can learn to understand your opponent's stratagems, his reasoning, his resources, and how to apply tactics to defeat them, you can beat anyone at any time.

An executive who wants to attain mastery in competitive situations can do so only by unremitting commitment. Train yourself and polish your skills day and night. After you have perfected your methods, you will gain a uniquely valuable freedom of action, a spontaneous ability to operate successfully even under the most arduous conditions, an ability to overcome the most difficult challenges. Your associates and your opponents will believe that you can perform miracles. And perhaps you can. This is what happens when you become a master competitor.

Competitive Position

Always occupy the most powerful position available. Look down on your opponent.

In a face-to-face conflict, look around carefully. Positioning is an important aspect in gaining strength. Sit with the light to your back. If the other person must squint, he will be unsettled.

In a closed room, make sure you are comfortable and have space to move freely. Do not allow yourself to be crowded or pushed around. Be aware of your position. Do not allow an opponent to stand behind you.

At night, make sure you can see your opponent. If the light is behind you, you can see him, but he will not be able to see you very well. These ideas may seem trivial or silly when they are read for the first time. But do not dismiss them until you have thought carefully and tried them out. In a hard situation, sometimes small advantages can make the difference between success and failure.

OPENING MOVES AND INITIATIVE

During a negotiation, make your opponent feel awkward. Put obstacles in the way of his arguments or strategies. Force him to trip over his own words. Place him at a disadvantage any way you can.

Keep the pressure on your opponent so he is more concerned with defending himself than watching where he is going. Do not let him see the danger he is in before he stumbles on it.

Every situation offers some kind of advantage. Use the factors available under the immediate circumstances to create a predominant position. Practice thinking about creating advantages from circumstances every day. Then you will be prepared in a crisis.

When a face-to-face conflict starts, there are three opening positions available. The first position is to attack your opponent before he attacks you (preemptive confrontation). Make your first move before your opponent makes his. The second position is to attack after your opponent attacks you (reactive confrontation). Wait until your opponent commits himself before responding. The third position is to attack at the same time as your opponent (mutual confrontation).

The person who has the initiative in a battle, who has momentum on his side, has the advantage. With initiative, it is possible to win a quick victory. Your first move determines whether you can gain the upper hand at the start. Hence, the first move is of great importance.

Each competitive situation has its own unique character. Learn ordered flexibility so that it is second nature to you and you can apply it instantly under pressure. Think about the particular situation you face. See the enemy's objectives and methods. Win by concentrating your strength and controlling the timing of your actions.

To seize the initiative in preemptive confrontation, first remain calm and quiet. Attack suddenly and quickly, without warning. Attack with energy, but leave yourself some reserve. Do not use yourself up in a frenzy; keep control. Strengthen your resolve when you close with your opponent. Move vigorously and swiftly the moment you get near enough to strike. Think only of crushing your opponent from start to finish. Empty your mind of everything except enthusiasm for victory and the will to win no matter what. Preemptive confrontation works best against a weaker or less confident opponent.

The second opening position is reactive confrontation. When your opponent attacks quickly and strongly, stay calm and unruffled. Pretend weakness. When your opponent gets close to you, move away suddenly. This will cause your opponent to hesitate for a moment. In that moment of hesitation, you must attack forcefully and grab the initiative from him. If you cannot move away from your opponent, then stay with him, returning his attack forcefully enough to disrupt his timing and cause him to change his approach. As soon as his timing is disrupted and you sense a change in approach, move quickly to take the initiative and seize victory. Reactive confrontation may be appropriate when facing an overconfident or careless opponent.

The third opening position is mutual confrontation. When an opponent attacks confidently, you attack calmly and strongly in the same moment. Identify a point of weakness and concentrate your strength on that point. When your opponent begins to defend his weakness and his attack slackens, defeat him immediately. Or if your opponent attacks smoothly and quietly, react flexibly. Match the pattern of his movements, then make a surprise feint. Watch his reaction. Use his reaction to defeat him. Mutual confrontation may be preferable when your strength is equal to your opponent or when you are uncertain about his resources.

Conflict situations are difficult to write about in detail. Your tactics must be fashioned in a moment, considering the specific conditions involved. The particular opening position you choose depends on circumstances. It is not necessary to be the first to attack. But you can only win a fight by taking the initiative away from your opponent. Therefore, getting and maintaining the initiative should be your first priority.

Whether you attack first or not, as soon as you have the initiative, you can win. Judging the most effective way to get the initiative is a function of your ability to assess the situation, concentrate your energy, and time your actions. Train yourself to think accurately in order to achieve victory.

It is especially dangerous in face-to-face conflict to allow your opponent to grab you by the nose and pull you wherever he wants you to go. No matter what else happens, to win a contest, you must gain control of your enemy's actions; you must be on the offensive and move about freely. This may not be easy. Your opponent will be thinking the same way as you are. But, if you can discern his method of attack, you can prevent him from gaining the initial advantage.

To win, you must parry your opponent's blows, stop his thrusts, and break his grip. Regardless of what your opponent does, when you have mastered competitive thinking, you will perceive and understand his approach. You will know in advance what moves he will make and defeat his attack before it begins.

The essence of the advantage conferred by ordered flexibility is to parry an opponent's blow at the letter "b"; to stop an opponent's thrust at the letter "t"; to break his grip at the letter "g". If you stop an action as it begins, the action can never defeat you.

An important idea in applying this method of winning is to understand the value and purpose of your opponent's maneuvers. Let him use up time and resources doing things that are useless. Prevent him from doing things that are useful. In this way you are able to preserve and concentrate your resources while he dissipates his own.

Reacting to your opponent's maneuvers is, however, essentially a defensive approach to conflict. When you are a master competitor, you will be able to stop an opponent's moves before they begin. You will be able to lead the opponent where you want him to go. You will strike him at the moment when you are strong and he is weak. To manipulate situations this way is a result of reflection and practice.

SITUATIONAL THINKING

In managing a business or organization, difficult situations and thorny problems occur frequently. These situations can be likened to crossing a wide expanse of ocean in a small boat.

A wide expanse of ocean can be safely crossed in a small boat if you research the currents along your chosen route; if you know the capabilities of your boat and crew; if you have access to a reliable weather forecast; if you are willing to make adjustments to your course based on prevailing conditions; and if you are determined to reach your destination whether the winds stay favorable or you must row your boat through storm and waves.

To be successful, you must apply the same attitude to solving the problems and winning the conflicts which occur each business day. Understanding your own resources is crucial.

Further, in business, it is important to assess correctly your competitor's resources, methods, and spirit. You must relate your own strengths to those of your competitor. In this way, you can cross a sea of difficulties safely, just as a skilled captain pilots his boat over the ocean.

To make the journey easier, put your competitor in a weaker position. Take the initiative yourself. Bend the situation to your purposes through unremitting strength of character. This approach works well whether you are involved in a large conflict with many participants or you are struggling one on one.

Once you have crossed over the sea, you can rest. But during the passage, you must constantly be alert.

Analyzing resources and environment allows you to understand the factors surrounding the conflict. From understanding the condition and intentions of your opponent, you can make appropriate decisions about deploying your own assets and your people. You can leverage your strength against his weakness and fight from a position of advantage. This is particularly important in conflicts involving larger numbers of participants.

When you are entangled in a conflict with another person or another group, your attitude must be that of understanding the present reality. Have no preconceived notions. Observe the character of your competitor, learn his method of approach, discover his expectations, plot the rhythm of his advances and retreats. Attack him at a time when he is unprepared, when his spirit is waning. This is critical to success.

If you stay focused on reality, you will comprehend the state of affairs which exists. You will recognize your competitor's intentions and attitudes. You will not be fooled or diverted into useless actions. You will see the path to victory and concentrate your efforts in the correct direction.

Tactics develop from specific conditions in the time and place of conflict. Only a fool assumes he will be able to follow the precise steps of a predetermined plan of action once the battle starts. The opportunities of the battlefield dictate tactics during a fight. Further, because communication and coordination are more difficult in situations of stress and chaos, tactics should be neither clever nor complicated. Straightforward actions executed quickly and confidently at an appropriate moment by the best people available create success.

DUELING

Most of the time, you cannot prevent your competition from striking at least one blow against you. The idea is to prevent him from striking a second. Parry the initial attack and then hold him down. In a sense, "step on his sword" so he cannot strike again.

If your tactics are designed only to parry your opponent's thrust, the battle will turn into sparring match.

You strike at him, he strikes at you, again and again. You will achieve nothing. Your tactics must overpower your competitor quickly so that he cannot strike again. Drawn-out conflicts waste resources and destroy morale.

Do not limit your tactics in any way. Use every available method of attack. If the competition senses your unyielding determination to win, this will destroy his spirit.

Unyielding determination means you are constantly trying to get the initiative. Follow up every opportunity vigorously and thoroughly. Be relentless and constant. Allow him no rest.

The idea is to cause the competition to collapse. All things collapse when their time comes and their rhythm is destroyed. It is important to sense your opponent's rhythm. When his rhythm begins to deteriorate, he becomes vulnerable. Do not miss this opportunity. If he recovers his rhythm, he can attack you again.

In every conflict, there is an opportunity for you to win. A loss of momentum or poise in the opponent's stance will signal your chance. Be ready to strike in this moment.

You must focus all of your energy on striking the enemy at his moment of vulnerability. Make your attack direct and powerful. Cut the enemy down so that he is completely unable to recover or continue. Remember, when you fight, fight to win. Do not allow your enemy a chance to beat you by being careless, sloppy, or foolish.

The Mind of the Enemy

See the situation from the competition's point of view. Think as the enemy thinks. Let me give you an example. If a dangerous criminal is cornered in a building, it is normal for the police outside the building to think of him as a powerful and difficult adversary. But if you look at the conditions from the criminal's point of view, he is trapped in a helpless position. A person hiding inside a surrounded building feels like a rabbit in a hole with no means of escape. People outside the building look to him like hawks poised for the kill. Consider this closely.

In situations where you are competing with large companies or powerful groups, it is natural to think of your competitors as powerful forces which must be handled carefully. But if you have good people on your side and carefully apply the principles of ordered flexibility, you will know how to beat the competition. Do not worry.

Put yourself in the mind of the enemy. Think about things from his perspective for a moment. As an exercise, think about it this way: What if you really believed your opponent were a master business competitor proficient in gaining advantages and a proven winner? Under those conditions, would you think that your chances of winning against him were high? On the other hand, if your opponent believes you are the master competitor, how much better would your chances be?

Deadlocks

When a contest between competitors becomes dead-locked and neither side is able to progress, it is necessary to give up on the tactics you are using and try something else. Deadlocked situations drain away precious resources. To break a deadlock, it is essential to use tactics which the competition does not expect.

Once the contest has begun to lag, you must judge the condition and spirit of the enemy. Change your aim. Attack from a place he is not watching. Throw him off balance with surprise.

Techniques

"Moving a shadow" refers to tactics you use when you cannot determine the enemy's position and design. For example, if it is impossible to discover the enemy's disposition or resources, you might pretend to make a strong attack at some point on his defenses. Watch how he maneuvers. This will tell you how he is thinking. Once you know how your opponent thinks, you can defeat him by devising an appropriate method.

In negotiation situations, people often give away their goals and tactics if you pretend to oppose them or interrupt their arguments with annoying or minor objections. Pay close attention to their reactions. Observe how they move and what they say. Feel the rhythm of the contest from their point of view. Are they anxious or confident? Chaotic or centered? Obvious or subtle? Once you know an opponent's state of mind, you have the advantage. Carefully time your attack to disrupt his rhythm. Do not miss your opportunity.

"Suppressing the spirit" is a tactic you can use when you sense that your opponent intends to attack. At the very moment the attack is to begin, emphatically demonstrate that you are willing and able to turn aside his advance. Overwhelm him with your enthusiastic response. When he hesitates or changes tactics, seize the initiative and overpower him.

This is another case of correctly perceiving your opponent's rhythm. When he attacks vigorously, if you can disrupt his attacking rhythm, he will be thrown off balance. As he pauses to regain his stance, time your response to take advantage of his moment of weakness. Watch carefully for your chance.

You can manipulate people by your actions. For instance, it is possible to make other people sleepy by acting sleepy yourself. You can induce others to yawn by yawning yourself. In a contest, you can influence an opponent's timing by the rhythm of your own actions.

If your competitor is excited, enthusiastic, or hurried, make a show of being calm and easy in your approach. This will influence your opponent to become less intense and to relax his pressure a little.

When you sense your competitor has matched your less hurried approach, instantly speed up your actions to catch him off guard. Let your opponent see that you are relaxed in body and in spirit. But as soon as he responds to your mood, attack with strength and speed to gain victory.

There are many other states of mind which can be passed on to your opponent. For instance, you can pass on boredom, carelessness, and timidity. Think about how you can use this in a fight.

It is also possible to upset the balance of your competition by using various tactics. One way is to put the competition under time pressure. Another is to create the impression of impending disaster or imminent danger. Another is to hint at the possibility of unknown or unexpected consequences.

Upsetting the other side is essential to victory. Come at your opponent, strongly and firmly, at a place or time or from a direction he is not expecting. Catch him unprepared and unaware. You will have the advantage while he is unsettled from your surprise attack. Use this moment to achieve your success.

A good way to upset a negotiating opponent is to change pace during a conflict. If you approach a situation slowly and then charge swiftly and forcefully, you will throw your opponent's mind into disarray. Do not allow a moment for your adversary to take a breath. Use this instant of hesitation as an opportunity to win.

It is not unusual for people to be afraid during situations where business conditions or structures are changing, for instance during major reengineering or downsizing projects, or where large amounts of money or organizational power are at stake. When outcomes are unknown, there is always concern about the future. When people are afraid, they are more vulnerable.

You can make your competition afraid in many ways. Methods that are not obvious or blatant are particularly useful because they work at an emotional level. You can frighten him with suggestions of loss. You can make a trivial point of concern seem quite important. You can threaten one of his weak spots. You can move quickly without warning. You can rush at him suddenly and then just as suddenly withdraw. Anything which creates fear, confusion, and surprise in the enemy's camp will give you the advantage.

When you are attempting to disrupt the enemy, you must maintain order and discipline within your group and within your own mind. The only way to do this is to practice. People who have not experienced the intense pressures of competition first hand on the practice field will always make mistakes in real situations. Without a doubt, uncertainty under pressure leads to defeat. In the heat of battle, you will act at a more instinctive, emotional level. Discipline your instincts and emotions beforehand. Your reactions in competition should be natural and precise, governed by an intellect sharpened through daily practice. Study hard; your future depends on it.

Remember, your best weapons in conflict are surprise and fear of the unknown. Use unexpected tactics to win. No tactic can be effective if your opponent knows about it beforehand. If you telegraph your moves to the enemy, he will be prepared for your attack. Unexpected tactics, however, cause concern and fear. Even if your opponent is larger and stronger than you are, if he is concerned and afraid, you will win.

This is why disciplined practice and study are critical to success in competition. Effective improvisation under the pressure of the moment decides the outcome of most conflicts. You will not have time to study or learn tactics in the midst of a battle. You can only use what you already know.

ATTACKING A STRONG DEFENSE

If your competitor has a strong defense, it will be difficult to attack him from the front. Under these circumstances, you should look for "cracks" in his defense. On the battlefield, a crack may be a gap or bulge in a line of soldiers. In business, a "crack" is any weakness, fault, or mistake in your opponent's presentation, arguments, position, or methods.

Cracks offer the opportunity to gain an advantage. Carefully observe your opponent's resources and programs. Concentrate on the less fortified areas. Less fortified areas are those which, for example, are staffed by less competent people, supported by fewer resources, or located in distant areas.

When an area of weakness begins to collapse, a feeling of panic and desperation will go through the entire enemy group. Follow up quickly when collapse begins and it may be possible to rout your opponent and defeat him immediately.

Against a strong opponent, you may have to whittle him down. Every time you engage him in conflict, injure him in some way. Do not let him escape unhurt, even if only a little. This will eventually deteriorate his physical strength, his economic resources, and his will to fight. In the end, winning is easy.

In order to apply these concepts in difficult situations, you must carefully analyze your opponent's position, resources, and objectives. Study him well.

CAUSING CONFUSION

Anything you can do to cause confusion is effective.

Never become predictable in competitive situations. Manipulate your competitor's impressions of you. Make him wonder. Where are you coming from? What are you doing? Are you in a hurry? Are you disinterested? Can you be trusted? Are you stupid? Use competitive tactics to confuse his mind. When your opponent gets caught up in chaotic speculation, you have certain success.

During the course of a negotiation, try various tactics and tricks as opportunities present themselves. Attack, retreat, change the subject, walk out of the room, take a phone call, postpone a meeting, arrive late, arrive early, ask a large number of detailed questions, leave early, leave late, forget something, change team members, feign illness. Do what you can to fluster the opposition. Of course, in business, you should use tactics which are appropriate to the nature of the situation. It is only necessary to win, not to embarrass oneself.

Business conflicts occur in offices and meeting rooms. They hardly ever involve physical violence. Rather than swords, the weapons of business are communication, information, money, influence, and technology. Gaining victory means gaining more power, position, or prestige. Failures are discouraging and inconvenient, perhaps expensive; but generally they are not fatal.

Nevertheless, there are serious consequences associated with carelessness and lack of composure.

Tactical Thinking

Applying the principle of ordered flexibility in competitive situations protects you from carelessness and inattention. Study your opponent carefully. Think about how you are related to each other. Think about his position. Is he your boss? An employee? A customer? A vendor? A client? A banker? A salesman? An associate? Another company? Another organization? The government? What type of person represents your competitor or challenger? What is his special competence? What is his background? What is the reason you are competing with each other? What is the reward for success? Is he afraid of loss or greedy for profit?

Using your experience, assess the other person's goals, objectives, and resources. If you were the other person, what would you be doing? You know your own situation much better than your opponent does. How could he defeat you if he knew what you know? What tactics would he use against you?

What economic, political, technological, social, and organizational conditions surround the contest? What impact could these have on the outcome of the contest? Who has the initial advantage? What is your opponent's character and habits? Have you grappled with him before? Does he telegraph his moves? Do you telegraph your moves? Take a moment to think about all these questions. Even if you are not sure of the answers, does it not seem beneficial to explore as many factors as possible to prepare yourself?

In a contest, think only in the present. See your situation in the moment. Do not worry about past assumptions or future consequences. The most effective tactic in battles of knowledge, power, and will is deception. Your opponent will surely try to use it. The most effective defense is confidence. Your opponent will surely try to steal your confidence.

During the contest, have no reservations about yourself, your knowledge, your product, or your organization. Question these beforehand or save them for later. Confident determination leads to victory. Strengthen your resolve.

Your adversary will sense your reluctance if you are afraid to act. Advance your position without hesitation. Once you are engaged, do not retreat.

It may not be possible to overwhelm your opponent in business situations. Winners and losers are not always clear cut in the office or marketplace. Concessions may be necessary. Partial victory may be the best you can achieve.

But, in order to gain anything, you must view yourself as strong, effective, resourceful. Keep a rein on your emotions. Loss of control leads to mistakes. This means that no matter who your opponent is, no matter how much or little is at stake, you expect victory. Take advantage of your competence and confidence. Concentrate your resources on profitable, attainable objectives.

When your opponent is not as competent or confident as you are, when your opponent is confused or distracted, when your opponent is tired or afraid, do not be foolish and let him recover his balance even a little. Seize the moment of victory.

Get this message into your heart.

During the course of a competitive situation, you will try many tactics. Sometimes you may repeat the same tactic twice. But if you repeat the same tactic more than twice, you become predictable. Predictability always spells defeat.

When a tactic does not work the first time you try it, do not rush to try it again. It probably will not work any better the second time. Change your approach. Try something different.

Winning in conflict requires, above all, mental flexibility. If your competitor thinks you will attack one way, then attack another. If he thinks you are far away, appear close at hand. Creating surprise is the expected result of applying the principle of ordered flexibility.

TOTAL VICTORY, TOTAL DEFEAT

Even if you think you have defeated your opponent, if he refuses to accept the fact he has been defeated, he may come at you again. Your enemy is defeated only when you have knocked the spirit out of him.

Make sure your opponent feels defeated from the bottom of his heart. Demoralize him as quickly and thoroughly as you can. Destroy his desire to win by any means possible. You have not really defeated him until he no longer has the will to fight.

Once you have crushed the competition's spirit, you do not have to worry about him. If he still harbors thoughts of victory, however, you will need to watch him over your shoulder. An opponent who retains his ambition is hardly defeated. If you are unsure of your victory, your celebration will be short lived.

RENEWAL

If you become entangled in a prolonged conflict and no resolution seems possible, you must throw away your current program and think about winning from a different perspective. Get back to the basics of ordered flexibility. Change your rhythm.

Modify your tactics. Try something new and different. Improvise based on the opportunity of the moment. Renew yourself. Renewal startles your opponent. In an instant you think differently and act differently.

When you get bogged down in details, for instance, shift your focus to the bigger issues. Do this suddenly and it will throw your opponent off track. The ability to switch from larger issues to smaller issues, or smaller issues to larger issues, is an integral part of winning tactics. Determining the right moment to change focus is a critical judgment. Practice this in all phases of your life to gain perspective.

Get into the mind of your competitor. See the issues and conditions of the conflict as he sees them. Once you do, you will be able to control him as if he were your servant. If you know his mind, you can move him wherever you like. This is the power of the master competitor.

Once you have attained the power of the master competitor, you will be able to win in all circumstances, using whatever tools are at hand. If you choose to be like a mountain — inaccessible, immovable, silent — then nothing can touch you. If you choose to be like the sea — flexible, fluid, free — then you can flow around your challengers and swallow them up.

What I have written above consists of issues and concerns which come up when one is trying to win the battles of business competition. It is difficult to write precisely about some of these issues because you can only master them by careful practice. In any case, the principles above can be used as a guide for someone who is interested in improving his skill.

The way of the master competitor is the science of winning in life, of getting the most benefit for yourself and for those to whom you owe a duty, no matter how you define this benefit. If you study ordered flexibility, practice it diligently, and apply it steadfastly, you will never have any doubt about your success.

5

FABRIC

THE CLOAK OF SUCCESS

To be successful in business-to-business competition, your employees must be able to select and execute appropriate tactics based on prevailing market, political, and economic conditions. Managing your organization well allows employees to execute actions effectively. In the Fabric chapter, I write about the characteristics of techniques for teaching competitive success and organizing larger groups of people, so that they can perform in difficult business situations.

When faced with a competitive situation, the idea is to respond effectively and appropriately given overall objectives. In most situations, there are several tactical choices available. Some of these choices are certainly better than others. But, often as not, the better choices are not obvious ones except after the fact. Effective tactics, like effective fabrics, are woven from elements that are simple, adaptable, and durable.

Every competitive situation involves uncertainty to a greater or lesser degree. If you adopt a method which is too structured for specific competitive circumstances, you will waste resources and time trying to control the uncontrollable. If you adopt a method which is too loose for circumstances, you will fail to control the controllable. If you go too far either way, you will be defeated.

Tactics are often thought of in a way that is limited to consideration of factors within the control of an organization. There are very few of these factors in any case. Further, control tends to be an illusion. Some executives believe that by using the latest theory or by creating a new type of structure, they can instantly produce desirable results. They believe new is always better. But if new theories or different organization structures do not enhance simplicity, adaptability, and durability, desirable results will not occur. In the next section, I will explain simplicity, adaptability, and durability, which are the three aspects of ordered flexibility that affect choices of organization structure and management style.

SIMPLICITY, ADAPTABILITY, AND DURABILITY

Simplicity facilitates understanding. Even if someone practices a technique every day, if he does not understand the purpose of the technique and how to apply it under different competitive circumstances, he will not be able to use it when a difficult situation arises.

Group understanding always tends toward the average. Some people in every group can absorb and comprehend almost anything, but most groups contain both more and less competent individuals. The strength of the group during a crisis or challenge is the strength of its least effective member. Therefore, keep your approach and structure as simple as possible. If the least knowledgeable person in your group understands his personal mission and how this fits into the whole, he will perform better. If the least knowledgeable person can also improvise effectively under conditions of uncertainty, you will inevitably achieve victory.

Adaptability fosters innovation. If people have mastered the details of a given technique through intense effort, but they do not understand the philosophy behind the technique and cannot adapt that philosophy to a specific situation, it will do little good in a crisis. Even a small misunderstanding can result in major errors in application.

Random events occur always and everywhere. Random events are always with us. And random events always result in unpredictable outcomes. Random events are not preventable because human beings lack complete understanding of the factors affecting the results of decisions. Make your approach and structure adaptable. Random events sometimes create wonderful opportunities. Be sure you can take advantage of them.

Durability encourages profitability. Buying a new wardrobe each year requires great expenditures of time and money. The time and money spent to select and acquire clothing is taken away from more enjoyable and valuable activities. Changing management techniques frequently increases cost and diverts people's attention away from the main objective of business — generating wealth for business owners.

THE WEAKNESS OF RIGIDITY

Some management philosophies depend heavily on rigid procedures and structured methods. From this point of view, they are difficult to start and, once started, momentum is difficult to sustain. Further, great attention is directed at creating the process in the first place. Problem identification and elaborately detailed plans are the main goals of these techniques. Effective execution of plans is not necessarily considered.

The conventional wisdom associated with rigid structure says that people can be managed through automatic processes in such a way that individual differences in ability are canceled out and control of results increased. The need for personal leadership is minimized. Everyone follows the process to success. This conventional wisdom reflects an ignorance of organizational reality. While processes do indeed provide order, they can also mask competence. Further, processes do not lead people. People lead people. In the end, it is a trained employee with the right tools, acting in a competent, cooperative, and reasonable manner, based on the facts of the situation, who produces profitable results.

If time is short and competition intense, highly structured processes are unwieldy and burdensome. They are not adaptable to rapidly changing circumstances. Moreover, they are not durable. They become obsolete as soon as competitive conditions change. And they are not simple to understand or implement.

The Weakness of Slack

On the other hand, there are philosophies of management and structure which rely heavily on individual or small group competence. Management methods involving empowerment or team building are examples of these philosophies. Both individual responsibility and small group performance are key elements in an organization's success. But does an incompetent or untrained person become better at his job if he is empowered? Can several incompetent or untrained persons create a masterpiece simply because they are working together in a group? As the philosopher Sun Pin once said: "A pig who escapes his pen is quickly lost. A headless snake writhes, but accomplishes nothing."

Empowerment is easy to talk about, but difficult to practice. Certain people can be empowered; others cannot. Unworkable systems will continue to be unworkable, even with empowered employees. Untrained or incompetent people remain so, even if placed in groups. Leaderless teams drift. Purposeless organization does not increase employee effectiveness. Useless activity wastes time and money. If people lack training, they cannot adapt. If organizations lack purpose, they will not endure. If leaders are absent, objectives will not be achieved.

ATTACKING WITH STRENGTH

Consider how to balance strength and weakness in conflict. There is no such thing as absolute strength or absolute weakness in competition. Everything is relative to circumstances. If you attack your opponent strongly, without at least challenging your assumption of superior strength, you may have difficulty in winning.

If you are intent on striking a strong blow when a strong blow is not appropriate for the circumstances, you may stumble into defeat. You accomplish the opposite of what you intend.

When you practice for conflict, it is a bad idea always to think about winning with strength. Sometimes cunning is necessary. Your strength can be used against you by a clever opponent.

When facing a difficult business situation, think only of success. Consider only what your organization is capable of. Let the circumstances shape your methods. Keep your mind focused on reality and the outcome you desire. Reliance on a rigid, predetermined set of tactics results in delay and disadvantage. Use an appropriate method at an appropriate time.

There is no such thing as an approach which can win in all situations. The fact of the matter is that your competition is just as smart, just as quick, just as capable as you are. Both sides have the same opportunity. Victory belongs to the one who uses the correct philosophy of competition.

When you use effective competitive thinking, you give no consideration to ideas or plans which are impossible for your group to achieve; the reality of the situation is all that matters. Use the power of facts to illuminate the path to victory.

No one tool, technique, teaching, or theory will work under every set of conditions. In practice, there is no one idea which has provided or will ever provide the final answer. Fondness for a particular approach is a fatal attraction. Defeat will follow.

A Defensive Approach

At the other end of the spectrum, there are people who always wait until an opponent exposes his weakness before striking. If applied indiscriminately, this approach is as dangerous as attacking too strongly. If your company is feinting, dodging, and responding all the time, you have adopted a defensive mindset. Defensive tactics may prolong the fight, but they seldom produce victory, particularly if your opponent is strong.

You may believe that a defensive mindset is safer. But all it does is allow you to be led around by the nose until your opponent gets tired of the sport. This will eventually demotivate your people. After that, your opponent will maneuver you into a death trap and finish you off.

Keys to Victory

The best way to win is to confuse the enemy about your true intentions. Sometimes you should adopt a defensive approach, sometimes an offensive one. Be ready to change. Make simplicity, adaptability, and durability your standards.

Remember, the way of victory lies in attacking weakness with strength. Surprise always causes confusion and fear. When you surprise your opponent, attack him quickly and destroy him. Facts prevent surprise. Listen to your first-line employees. They know more about what the competition is up to.

Most of what people are normally taught about tactics in the classroom amounts to learning how to jump about deftly, deflect advances, evade attacks, retreat when threatened, and generally get through things safely. They are also taught that there are right and wrong answers. Being safe and being correct becomes a habit. As a result, people usually end up getting manipulated and mauled by others. When you must fight, think only of winning by using the best available movement. A "safe" death is still a sure death. Give yourself a chance to win.

Because of the way people are taught, they sometimes believe that activity produces results. For example, some people believe that the number of hours one works is a measure of one's value. For this reason, some executives are overly impressed when outsiders propose improvement techniques which require lots of unnecessary meetings and many hours of unproductive activity. Methods which do not measurably improve bottom-line profits are false and foolish. Avoid them.

It is a delusion to think that there is any secret formula or technique for success in competitive situations. The essence of all success is a practical combination of straightforward methods. Cut down your enemy quickly and directly. Excessive movements or fancy sword thrusts only give your enemy the opportunity to stab you through the heart.

The objective of competition is to win. There is no need to get cute. You may face challenges or obstacles. Keep your mind focused so you can deal with them. Analyze resources, environment, attitude, concentration, and timing. Create a simple, adaptable, and durable method of keeping focused.

Adding complications to the process of fighting is unwise. You will not kill your opponent by twisting your hands a certain way, twirling your body around, jumping about vigorously, or leaping back and forth. Twisting, twirling, jumping, and leaping just work up sweat. Otherwise, they are totally useless. Focus only things that produce desirable results. Gain victory by causing your opponents to twist, twirl, jump, leap, and generally waste energy. Attack at a time when your opponent is off balance, confused, and afraid. Examine this idea well.

TRAINING PEOPLE TO WIN

When you and your organization train for conflict, do not be rigid in teaching people how to act. Training situations tend to be simplified, tailored versions of reality. Techniques used in training cannot be presented as if they are the only way to accomplish a task.

Even though, for discussion purposes, you can prescribe standard solutions to competitive situations, the fact is that conditions in real battle are always different from the conditions used as examples in training.

Indeed, training for the next battle usually consists of fighting the last battle over again. The tactics which succeeded in last year's marketing campaign, for instance, are already obsolete. The key to victory is simple: Put the enemy at a disadvantage. Attack weakness with strength. There are many ways to do this.

Standard solutions induce an attitude in people that there are easy ways to win or that one can make oneself invincible. This is far from the truth. Standard solutions give people the idea that there is only one way to do things. This idea inevitably leads to difficulty and defeat.

Victory in real-life battles is won by seizing the initiative through careful thinking and bold movement at the right moment. The standard solutions taught in training are best considered as starting points for discussion of alternatives. In other words, say to people: "Start here and evolve according to circumstances." Carefully consider how you might do this.

Conventional and Unconventional Methods

Sun Tzu, the great Chinese military philosopher and general, said: "Approach the enemy in conventional formation, but win the battle by unconventional means." This is the heart of ordered flexibility. Set up your organization so that it approaches competitive challenges in an organized, disciplined manner, but is not limited in its choice of maneuvers. Your enemy will think you are a conventional opponent. Then throw him off balance by unconventional tactics. When he is confused and irritated, overwhelm him.

In pitched battles between large organizations, it is of the greatest importance to base your initial position on clear, factual analysis. For example, how many and what type of troops does the enemy employ? (Resources.) What is the structure of the battlefield? (Environment.) Is the enemy's morale high? (Attitude.) What are the strong and weak points of the enemy's strategy and structure? (Concentration.) Is your enemy's rhythm fast or slow? (Timing.) After you have considered these aspects, begin the battle.

Gaining the initiative is critical to success and should be a paramount consideration in the early stages of battle. After you have lost the initiative, it is very difficult to regain it. The morale and motivation of employees are fed by action. Waiting for the enemy to attack fosters fear and depression. Confidence and excitement create enthusiasm. Enthusiasm powers success.

PERCEIVING REALITY

Observe the enemy's activities closely, but do not allow your group to fix on one particular aspect of his movements. It is a common tactic in battle to distract an opponent with a flurry of activity in one place and then attack strongly in other. Notice details and retain a sense of the whole at the same time. This takes practice.

Basketball players can dribble the ball, pass it, catch it, and shoot it without appearing consciously to watch the ball. This is because they have thoroughly trained their movements. When you are thoroughly trained, it is possible to see everything at the same time, even while you are performing other specific tasks. A skilled juggler can manage a large number of flying objects without concentrating on any one of them. He feels the rhythm in the movement of the objects as a whole. He adjusts his hands and feet in response to that rhythm without dropping anything. Constant practice allows him to "concentrate without fixation."

When you face an opponent, assess the weight of his sword and the strength of his arm. More importantly, see into his heart and perceive his spirit and his will. Strength of spirit and power of will determine the enemy's ability to sustain the fight.

To win in any conflict, large or small, there can be no such thing as a narrow focus. When you narrow your focus to insignificant details, you lose the perspective of the whole. Opportunities will escape your grasp. Train yourself to perceive with the mind.

Seeing with the eyes and perceiving with the mind are two different ways of observing situations. The seeing eye can be fooled; the perceiving mind cannot. Observe the nature of the situation, the state of the enemy, the rhythm of the conflict. Keep your people focused broadly. Perceive the progress of the conflict, feel the ebb and flow of morale, watch for your moment of victory. This is the surest way to win.

FANCY FOOTWORK

Practicing certain predetermined movements or fancy maneuvers at the beginning of the conflict is dysfunctional. This is like trying to use fancy footwork in sword fighting.

Fancy footwork tends to cause one to lose one's balance or to lose the initiative. Fancy footwork is fine in a dance contest. In real combat, it is a dance of death.

Hopping, floating, or leaping tends to put one in an awkward position. These maneuvers create a sense of excitement among people, causing them to lose focus. There is an attitude of trying to execute the movement rather than win the battle. This is dangerous.

Being unnecessarily stubborn is another useless maneuver. Stubbornness puts you on the defensive and takes away the initiative. You allow your opponent to strike the first blow. This is also dangerous.

The nature of conflict is such that battle often occurs under difficult conditions. Depending on the circumstances, it may not be possible to step or maneuver around in a specific pattern. It's like fighting a duel in a swamp, or on a rocky hilltop, or along a narrow forest path.

The pattern of maneuvers used in the beginning of a conflict should not be predetermined. Instead, approach conflict the way you approach everyday activity. Perceive the rhythm of your opponent. Move quickly or slowly according to the needs of the situation. Be orderly in approach, but flexible in response.

An overly rigid or slack organization will not allow this to happen.

RHYTHM

Perception of the enemy's spirit and will is essential to timing your advances. If you become too hurried and attack prematurely, you may find yourself in disorder. If you are too slow and methodical, you can lose the opportunity to beat the opponent when he is demoralized and confused. If timing is wrong, you will not be able to attain a quick victory.

It is absolutely necessary to correctly judge the moment when an opponent begins to doubt himself and his defenses begin to crumble. Train your employees to strike in this moment. Give the competition no time to recover.

Timing movements in conflict requires neither an attitude of speed nor an attitude of slowness. Rather, the attitude is one of sensing the rhythm of the conflict.

The master competitor moves neither fast nor slow. A skilled runner can run all day, but he never appears to change his stride. An unconditioned runner may also run all day, but he will never reach the finish line.

If an orchestra mixes skilled with unskilled musicians when playing a symphony, there will be a sense of either dragging or hurrying in their performance. Skilled musicians always play a piece in the correct tempo, whether fast or slow, and the music will sound appropriate because the rhythm is matched to the score. Highly expert performers never run out of time. Their actions are neither rushed nor lax. Experienced people are never too busy, nor do they miss deadlines.

The habit of speed is particularly bad during competition or negotiating. Depending on the circumstances encountered, it may not be possible, appropriate, or necessary to move quickly. If there are large sums of money or important issues at stake, when you rush to cut to the heart of the matter, you may end up cutting nothing except yourself. Cut the appropriate thing at the appropriate moment. If you move too quickly, you may stumble and break your nose. If you move too slowly, you will lose the advantage. You must learn this well.

If you approach a conflict with the idea of seizing the right moment, you will never be too fast or too slow. If the dance is a tango, then perform a tango. If the dance is a waltz, then perform a waltz. Your dance will succeed if you are in rhythm with the music. This philosophy must be transmitted throughout the entire organization.

If your opponent is in a hurry, you can use it against him. Match his haste with detachment. Remain calm and unmoved. Do not be manipulated to talk or act faster than you want.

Straight and Clear

Managing people using the way of the master competitor is neither secret nor complex. Winning in conflict, negotiation, and competition is a direct and straightforward affair. Management structure and approach must be simple, adaptable, and durable. People must be adequately organized, but not constrained.

Teaching your group to be master competitors takes time and commitment. Begin with a clear framework. As your people gain experience, delve deeper into the nuances of competitive assessment and tactics. There is no such thing as beginning or advanced knowledge. There is only practice. Practice until the points I have made here become second nature to everyone. You will become more skilled in the process. These ideas are not intellectual or complex. But, you must act on them to understand them.

It is like digging a tunnel into a mountain. If you dig deeply enough, you will come out the other side. Through practice and teaching, your personal understanding will increase until conscious awareness of your mastery disappears.

There is no need to make my teachings mysterious or complicated. Take what is here at its face value. Do what I suggest according to your ability and understanding. The way to win will open for you and your organization if you train and practice seriously together.

6

Focus

In the previous four chapters, I have written about the philosophy of ordered flexibility. The essence of the master competitor is, while based on ordered flexibility, more subtle and comprehensive than any single method or philosophy. The master competitor works at a level beyond conscious thought because he has trained himself thoroughly. I call this level "focus within focus." On this level, he knows how to act without the need to reconsider method or philosophy.

Beyond theory, beyond speculation, beyond philosophy, there is the reality of competition. In competition, you win or lose, live or die. If you know how to compete, you know how to survive and prosper.

Many people misunderstand the nature of competition. Competition is joyful; it is a fundamental process of life itself. In order to truly live, one must compete. The specific type of competition is immaterial;

compete against yourself, compete against others, compete against God. It is not important. Pick something you are interested in. What really counts is wanting to do something well.

If you choose the path of competition (in truth, which of us has a real choice?), you must work at understanding the rules of winning in order to do well. Do not become confused by unnecessary complexities or false expertise.

Master competitors study their craft accurately and diligently. They do not question the necessity for study, nor delude themselves into carelessness. Once you have decided to follow this path, you must practice every day. Learn to perceive the heart of your enemy, the essence of your challenge. When there is "focus within focus," the clouds of uncertainty and confusion disappear.

People who do not understand the path of competition very well probably think that their own methods, however superficial, are correct and solid. But I challenge you to look at the lives and actions of master competitors (like those discussed in the next part of this book). These people are not common fools wandering around lost in a fog, stumbling on success by accident.

The heart of success is perceiving the reality of situations and doing appropriate things at appropriate moments. No matter what you tell yourself, reality exists anyway. Function within this truth and you cannot fail. See things as they are and win. This requires practice. This requires courage.

Move towards mastery in a straightforward way. Practice honestly. Learn everything you can. Think clearly. Make "focus within focus" your goal and the path will open up to you.

In "focus within focus," there is effectiveness, not failure; strength, not weakness. Wisdom speaks; logic rules; principle guides; excellence prevails. Order and flexibility work together. The way of the master competitor is clear. The mind is calm. Reality governs action.

PART III
BATTLE TACTICS FOR BUSINESS

7

GAINING COMPETITIVE ADVANTAGE

Musashi's philosophies have been used by the world's most successful business executives and military generals to win in competition in the marketplace and on the battlefield. In this chapter, I will give you a number of examples so you can begin to think about how to apply Musashi's ideas and principles in your own situation. The examples I have chosen are:

— Howard Schultz (Starbucks Coffee)
— General Robert E. Lee and the Battles of Chancellorsville and Gettysburg
— Warren Buffett
— General George Washington and the Battle of Trenton
— Andy Grove (Intel)
— Bill Gates (Microsoft)

— Lawrence of Arabia and guerrilla warfare in
   Arabia
— Donald Trump
— The Battle of Rorke's Drift in the Zulu War in
   Africa

Musashi's principles have real value in winning competitive situations if they are applied correctly. The examples I have chosen here are designed to present various aspects of competitive situations and explain how the competitive situations were affected and enhanced using Musashi's ideas. I believe that there is something in each one of these examples which can help you gain an immediate advantage.

In my own business (consulting), I have discovered that the competitive situations I face often resemble those faced by others in the past. (There is an old saying: "If you learn from someone else's mistakes, you will not have to learn from your own.") If I haven't personally used a given tactic or approach before, but I am familiar with a similar situation that someone else has faced, I can usually apply the same reasoning, at least as a starting point.

The people and situations described below may help you do the same thing. Look for similarities and then work out how to use the strategies in your own mind. Remember to use the framework of the seven principles to anchor your thinking process. If you practice enough, as Musashi suggests, the analysis will come automatically. I believe that this will dramatically improve your understanding of competitive situations and your evaluation of alternatives. This understanding will ultimately give you the winning edge.

HOWARD SCHULTZ — STARBUCKS

How does someone turn a commodity product like a cup of coffee into a multibillion-dollar worldwide corporation? Howard Schultz suggests you "pour your heart into it." (See his book *Pour Your Heart Into It*, Hyperion, New York, 1997. All quotes in this section are from this book.)

Schultz pours his heart into his business in two ways. First, he sends a strong signal about the attitudes required for success through his example of ethical leadership. Second, he shares his love of coffee and his drive for serving the customer with every member of his organization. The sharp edge of Starbucks' competitive sword is a passion for service.

An attitude of ethical leadership is the foundation of a passion for service. Here is what Schultz says about ethical leadership: "Whatever your culture, your values, your guiding principles, you have to take steps to inculcate them in the organization early in its life so that they can guide every decision, every hire, every strategic objective you set. Whether you are CEO or a lower level employee, the single most important thing you do at work each day is communicate your values to others, especially new hires. Establishing the right tone at the inception of an enterprise, whatever its size, is vital to its long-term success."

Shared values are the cornerstone of competitive success in leading large numbers of people. Shared values spin a web of expectations which people can use to anchor their decisions and actions. Shared values encourage trust between management and employees. And trust is the mortar that holds together the bricks of an enterprise. Where trust is strong, organizations can easily prosper. Schultz adds: "There is no more precious commodity than the relationship of trust and confidence a company has with its employees. If people believe management is not fairly sharing the rewards, they will feel alienated. Once they start distrusting management, the company's future is compromised."

What is Starbucks' competitive advantage? How does it earn a premium profit on a commodity product? There are several elements to its success, according to Schultz — great coffee, great service, great atmosphere. But the most important element is the attitude of employees, an attitude which transmits excitement, optimism, passion for service, and a love of the product to the customer. Schultz has worked hard to develop this kind of attitude in his company. He suggests that setting an example is critical to transmitting a positive, winning attitude in his associates. He says: "The only way to win the confidence of Starbucks' employees was to be honest with them, to share my plans and excitement with them, and then to follow through and keep my word, delivering exactly what I promised — if not more. No one would follow me until I showed them with my own actions that my promises were not empty."

Starbucks' competitive sword is simple to understand. If you love coffee, you will love Starbucks, because it loves serving coffee to you. Employees at Starbucks generally like and trust their company. People appreciate a fine product served to them in a convenient location exactly the way they want it by enthusiastic employees. It is the friendly environments and bright smiles, it is Howard Schultz's attitude of confidence transmitted through his organization, that bring the same people back day after day. The secret of Starbucks' competitive sword is this: Customers will pay a premium price and buy more often if they feel good while they are doing it. Simple to understand? Yes. Easy to achieve? No. Ethical behavior and positive attitude are important elements of Musashi's philosophy. Howard Schultz uses them effectively to succeed at Starbucks.

GENERAL ROBERT E. LEE

Military events of the American Civil War from the Southern perspective make an excellent study for executives fighting for survival in markets where their companies are not the dominant players. (In other words, the great majority of us.) The Southern Confederate forces were always at a disadvantage in terms of resources and manpower. The Union had more money, more weapons, and more men. The Confederate army in Virginia, particularly, offset the Union's advantage by aggressiveness, morale, confidence, and speed. This was characteristic of General Robert E. Lee's strategic philosophy. Lee was commander of the Confederate Army of Northern Virginia. His approach to tactics has been described as defensive–offensive, which is the military embodiment of ordered flexibility. That is, remain on the defensive until your opponent offers you an opportunity. Then, strike quickly and strongly.

Two battles fought in the summer of 1863 — the Battle of Chancellorsville and the Battle of Gettysburg — illustrate the importance of Musashi's seven principles of competitive success. The same two armies participated in both battles. The Battle of Chancellorsville was an overwhelming victory for the Southern forces and a tribute to the quality of the Confederate army.

The Battle of Gettysburg was, at best, a marginal military victory for the Union, but it was, nonetheless, an enormous political victory. As a result of the battle, the South was not able to force the North into a negotiated solution to the war. Winning on the negotiation table was the only way the Confederacy could have survived in the long run. But a military victory on the battlefield at Gettysburg was necessary in order to provide the political leverage. The difference in the outcomes of these two battles can be analyzed in terms of Musashi's principles.

The Battle of Chancellorsville was fought in May 1863. In December 1862, General Lee had defeated the Union forces under General Burnside at Fredericksburg. Lincoln replaced Burnside with General Joe Hooker, a West Point graduate. Lincoln badly needed a commanding general who would fight rather than just train and maneuver. Hooker had the reputation of being a fighter.

During the winter months of 1862–3, the two opposing armies faced each other across the river at Fredericksburg, Virginia. Hooker's plan was to move a significant force around the rear of the Confederate army in the spring of 1863 and catch the Confederates between the Union forces holding Fredericksburg and his own troops behind them. This, Hooker thought, would pressure General Lee to retreat towards Richmond so he would not be attacked from two directions. Hooker had more than 70,000 men in the force moving towards the rear of the Confederate army and another 40,000 at Fredericksburg in front. Lee had a total of 60,000 men, so he was outnumbered almost 2 to 1. Because of numerical superiority, General Hooker was very confident that his battle plan would work.

On May 1, 1863, General Hooker attacked Lee as planned. But because he had sent his entire cavalry force on a mission away from the battlefield towards Richmond as a diversion, Hooker had no information about the enemy's movements. Without information, in the midst of what appeared later to be a successful attack, Hooker hesitated, lost his nerve, and withdrew his troops back into their previous lines. This set the stage for Lee's spectacular attack on May 2, 1863.

Hooker settled his 70,000 men around Chancellorsville on the night of May 1. Because Lee had a superb cavalry under J. E. B. Stuart, he knew where the Union army was camped and how they were disposed. The Union troops directly facing Lee were strongly positioned with a river on their left flank. The right flank and rear were, however, exposed. It is easy to suppose that General Hooker was so confident of victory, because of numerical superiority, that he felt there was no danger of Confederate attack on his right flank (which was actually behind him to the west).

At dawn on May 2, General Stonewall Jackson and 26,000 men (almost half of Lee's effective force) began marching south around the Union army position. When dust from this movement was spotted by Union observers, General Hooker assumed that Lee was retreating. Instead of retreating, Stonewall marched all the way around Hooker's camp and hit the right rear of the Union army at 6 p.m., routing the men. The attack was totally unexpected and beautifully managed. Lee and the Confederate army won because they obtained accurate information, focused strength on weakness, and executed appropriate tactics at an appropriate moment.

Here are the factors which gave the outnumbered Confederates a victory: Lee and Jackson were a battle-tested team. Hooker was newly appointed and had not been commanding general before. Hooker's cavalry was elsewhere during the battle. J. E. B. Stuart provided Lee with up-to-date and accurate information. Because of the information, Lee was able to concentrate his attack on the Union army's unprotected and vulnerable right rear. Stonewall Jackson had trained and organized his troops so they could move quickly and strike boldly. They marched around the Union army and then attacked in the evening of the same day; there were no delays and no hesitation. Lee and Jackson followed Musashi's principles and succeeded. Unfortunately for the Confederate army, Stonewall Jackson was wounded by his own men during the battle and died a few days later.

The Battle of Gettysburg was fought two months later, July 1–3, 1863, by the same armies. In this battle, the balance of competitive advantage shifted to the Union forces, causing a Confederate defeat. After Chancellorsville, the Union army moved to protect Washington, D.C. with the Confederate army following. But Lee's men were running low on supplies. Hence, the Confederates decided to invade Pennsylvania. The North was rich with supplies that were desperately needed by Southern soldiers. Further, an invasion would apply military pressure and perhaps compel the Union to negotiate an end to the war.

Lee reorganized his army because of Stonewall Jackson's death. He promoted the best generals he had into command of his divisions, but they were neither as experienced nor as effective as Jackson. Before moving into Pennsylvania, Lee split his army into several parts. He did this to allow his men to obtain the maximum amount of badly needed supplies and material. The Battle of Gettysburg started when a unit of Lee's army moved towards Gettysburg on July 1, 1863, looking for a large quantity of shoes which were supposed to be stored in the town.

Although Lee's forces won a decisive victory on the first day of the three-day battle, Lee was unable to follow up his initial advantage because he lacked accurate information; he did not concentrate strength on weakness; and his commanders executed tactics poorly. J. E. B. Stuart and his cavalry were not on the battlefield until the third day of the battle. Lee had sent Stuart ahead of him into Pennsylvania, and Stuart, for some reason, did not remain in close contact with Lee. The information Lee needed about the size of the Union army and its disposition were lacking. He did not know the details of the forces opposing him at Gettysburg.

Lacking specific information, Lee could not concentrate his attack on enemy weakness. He tried attacking at various points across the Union front in the hope of finding an opportunity, but because he could not concentrate, his attacks did not accomplish the desired result.

Further, the newly appointed Confederate commanders were not experienced enough nor bold enough to continue the attacks once the initial advantage had been gained. Several of them hesitated at crucial moments on both the first and second days of the battle, losing opportunities to gain an advantage. (I would like to note that boldness and initiative are two of the main strengths of highly effective business executives. Gates and Trump come to mind quickly.)

Lee and his chief lieutenant, General James Longstreet, disagreed on tactics for the battle. Longstreet did not want to attack the strong Federal defensive positions. Rather, he wanted to maneuver the Confederate army towards Washington and force the Union army to attack him. As a result of the disagreement, Longstreet seemed to drag his feet at crucial points in the battle, again losing valuable time and blunting initiative. The impact of Longstreet's reluctance to follow orders on the outcome of the battle is a matter of considerable debate, even today. Lee himself was quoted in later years as saying that he would have won the battle if Jackson had been there.

Anyone who leads people in highly competitive situations needs to learn two important lessons from Lee's defeat at Gettysburg. First, one superbly talented person can make a difference — the Michael Jordan principle. Second, every team member, regardless of talent, needs to make their best effort after decisions are made.

Lee's generals did not execute well, particularly with respect to timing. Attacks, when they occurred, were late and in the wrong places. At times, there did not seem to be much vigor and energy in the Confederate attempts. By the third day, Lee was deadlocked and could not continue the battle. He was forced by circumstances (not military defeat) to retreat back towards Maryland on July 4, 1863.

WARREN BUFFETT

Successful people seem to take similar approaches to competitive success. Like General Lee, Warren Buffett uses information as his primary competitive tool and timing as his primary tactical maneuver.

As a young man, Warren Buffett made two startlingly simple observations. First, he observed that the way people value stocks in the short run was based on the alternating emotions of greed for profit and fear of loss. Fear and greed caused stock values to fluctuate above and below their objectively determinable intrinsic values.

His second observation was equally important. High-quality stocks which had been depressed below their objectively determinable intrinsic values by short-run fears were better long-term investments. They had a higher probability of gain.

Having made these two simple observations, Buffett centered his attention entirely on four critical competitive elements to make his fortune. First, he became an expert at using available information to determine the intrinsic value of stocks. Second, he applied his attention to a small group of industries so he could become an expert in determining the value of potential investments. Third, he developed a workable method for timing his transactions. Fourth, he practiced self- discipline. These four competitive elements operating together over an extended period resulted in billions of dollars of wealth. Let's look at the elements of Buffett's competitive sword (i.e., information, timing, and self-discipline) more closely.

Warren uses information to determine an objective intrinsic value for a business. A business is valuable to Buffett when the projected annual compound rate of return on his investment exceeds a certain value. That value is reported to be 15 percent. There is a huge amount of data available to investors these days. But information is created only when some kind of knowledge is uncovered through appropriate analysis of data. Hence, Buffett first gains knowledge from data by becoming thoroughly familiar with certain industries. He does not even look at companies in industries which are outside his "circle of competence." (This is an excellent example of the use of focus.) Second, within these selected industries, Buffett invests only in companies whose earnings streams are reasonably predictable and whose market position and cost structure are strong. A strong market position and cost structure are evidenced by consistently high returns on shareholders' equity, high market share, the existence of barriers to entry for potential competitors, and a management team that is shareholder value oriented.

Warren selects his acquisition targets and then waits until the price he must pay to acquire an investment allows him to earn his target return. The stock market, as a whole, is not highly objective in setting the prices of stock shares. While the price one pays or receives for stock is a reflection of the supply and demand for the stock at a given moment, the price is not necessarily related to an objectively determined intrinsic value. Emotion is a strong influence on the point-of-the-moment value of stocks. The impact of emotion on stock prices causes prices to fluctuate considerably over even short periods of time.

In general, an average stock traded on the New York stock exchange fluctuates 20 to 30 percent in value each year. The ideal investment strategy would invest money at low points in the annual price cycle. This is what Buffett has been able to do. By using information to target certain companies and by setting target acquisition prices which will yield expected rates of return, Buffett has developed a workable timing system. This system will not be infallible, but it does give him a greatly increased probability of earning a profit and a greatly diminished chance of losing money.

According to research done on Buffett's results, a significant portion of the money he earns can be attributed to a relatively small number of the investment decisions. If one were to eliminate the big winners, Buffett's returns are only mediocre. Self- discipline makes the difference. He has the discipline to ride the winners and dump the losers. If an investment is not performing well (based on objective intrinsic value analysis), it is removed from the portfolio. If an investment meets the objective criteria, it stays, regardless of what price the highly emotional stock market assigns to it at a given moment.

What is Buffett's competitive sword? Buffett analyzes data to create usable information. With the information, he selects industries and companies which meet certain objective criteria as investment targets. He times his acquisition of these companies based on measurable economic and business factors. Finally, he does not react to short-term fluctuations in stock prices. Hence, Buffett applies Musashi's principles of information, timing, and self-discipline.

GENERAL GEORGE WASHINGTON

As we have seen, boldness and initiative are common characteristics of both successful military leaders and business executives. Boldness and initiative are especially needed when a competitive situation is deteriorating. Gaining the initiative in a fight, particularly against a stronger opponent, is immensely important. But executing bold tactics from a position of relative weakness requires careful use of Musashi's principles.

The situation facing General George Washington in late December, 1776, was rapidly getting worse. His small and badly equipped army was about to melt away because many enlistments were expiring on December 31. The pay and conditions were so bad that none of the volunteers wanted to stay and fight for independence. He needed to revitalize morale by winning a victory. Washington selected the Hessian garrison at Trenton, New Jersey as his point of attack. Here is how he would have used Musashi's REACT principles (resources, environment, attitude, concentration, timing) to plan and execute tactics for this battle.

Washington had three important resources at this critical time (December, 1776). First, he had an army of about 6000 men which would shrink to 1200 after January 1, 1777. The men required to do the job were trained and available for the next few weeks. Second, he had information. Washington knew where the British were stationed. It was winter and the main British army had entered its winter quarters in New York. Across areas controlled by the British, there were garrisons of troops, but the garrisons were small and separated by too great a distance to allow them to reinforce each other quickly. Therefore, he could attack with superiority of numbers in specific locations if he surprised the enemy. Third, he had boats. Between Washington's army and the New Jersey shore was the Delaware River. Washington had a fleet of flatboats which were ideal for moving men and equipment across a river. Further, his army had experience in using these boats for transport.

The main environmental factors were the weather and the time of the year. Washington assumed correctly that the British would not expect a major attack on the day after Christmas. The day of the attack turned out bitterly cold with blowing snow. Even though this type of weather was difficult to move around in, it was ideal for surprise.

Attitude played a significant role in Washington's success. The British were smug in their belief that the American army could not attack in winter, or if they did, the British would easily defeat them. Washington knew that the British general in charge of the garrisons in New Jersey held the American army in contempt. As a result, the British were careless in their defensive preparations. The Americans, on the other hand, had a "do or die" attitude towards the battle. If Washington's army did not win a quick victory, the American revolution could end. The rebels had nothing to lose and everything to gain by swift, aggressive action. (This is an important consideration if you find yourself with the upper hand in a competitive situation. Musashi tells us that an enemy is not defeated until he no longer has the desire to fight. If you win a battle, win it thoroughly and completely. Do not underestimate your opponent or you may find yourself in the same position as the British.)

Washington concentrated his ragged army against the even smaller force of Hessian mercenaries garrisoned in Trenton. Although the British outnumbered him greatly in total forces in the region, this approach gave him local superiority. Washington's plan of attack called for three units to attack Trenton from different directions. In this way he would prevent any of the garrison from escaping.

Washington marched his men towards Trenton, New Jersey, on Christmas Day, 1776. He expected (correctly) that the British would be inattentive on that day. Although he did have the larger force of men at the point of attack, Washington's most powerful weapon was surprise. He moved his men on Christmas night across the Delaware River and marched through the night to Trenton for an early morning attack on December 26.

Washington's forces completely surprised the Hessians. In fact, Washington lost only two men in this battle, both of whom froze to death when they stopped during the march for rest. The victory at Trenton revitalized American military operations.

In competitive business situations, it is important to keep the factors of success in front of you at all times using a tool like the REACT principles. If you are stronger in a situation, complacency and carelessness with regard to your competitors lead to surprise, embarrassment, and defeat. On the other hand, if you are weaker, reviewing the factors of competition may reveal unexpected opportunities for profit. Although victory in battle goes more often to the side with greater assets, this is true only if both sides are equally prepared. If the weaker side is more informed and active than the stronger side, it is possible for the weaker side to win.

ANDY GROVE — INTEL

Andy Grove, CEO of Intel and *Time* magazine's 1997 Man of the Year, provides a sterling example of how to use Musashi's principles to achieve outstanding results in a competitive high-technology business. In his book *Only the Paranoid Survive* (Currency, New York, 1996), he tells about the circumstances, decisions, and actions involved in Intel's decision to de-emphasize its memory business and devote its resources to developing and manufacturing microprocessors.

By 1985, the Japanese memory chip manufacturers had obtained more than a 50 percent share of the memory chip market. They did this in two ways. First, they used their competitive sword of manufacturing quality and process improvement to develop higher-quality memory chips which could be produced at a lower cost than those of American manufacturers, including Intel. Second, they used their quality/cost advantage and aggressive marketing tactics to drive down memory prices. In effect, they turned computer memories into a commodity product. Economics for commodity businesses favor the low-cost producer. The Japanese have successfully used this tactic over and over again.

According to Grove, Intel was faced with three choices in response to the growing Japanese challenge. First, Intel could try to out-duel Japanese manufacturers by creating more economies of scale and subsequently lowering production cost (i.e., low-cost strategy). In this way, Intel would end up the low-cost producer, at least for a short while until the Japanese responded. Second, Intel could look for niche markets for which the company would produce special-purpose memory chips that could be sold at a premium profit (i.e., niche strategy). In this way, Intel would maintain its profit margins, but it might sacrifice volume, total profitability, and growth rate, not to mention share price. Or, third, Intel could try to innovate in order to produce a branded, non-commodity product which the Japanese could not duplicate easily (i.e., product innovation strategy). In this way, Intel could maintain both profit and volume, but the risk of failure was relatively high.

The company chose the third option, to innovate its product. In implementing this decision, the company's management superbly utilized the philosophy of ordered flexibility coupled with leadership and timing.

Intel's upper management spent months preparing and convincing company employees and executives to move in a new direction. They maintained the current order while paving the way for change. Groves writes that this was a difficult task. People within the company were passionately attached to the existing product structure. They were not anxious to change. But Grove provided stable leadership and clear direction.

However, he adds, it is not enough to be clear and stable. He also recommends experimentation, that is flexibility, during challenging times. Yesterday's solutions do not necessarily fit today's problems. Yet, today's executives have succeeded using yesterday's methods. Flexibility is absolutely necessary to overcome challenges. If a company is experiencing rigidity in thinking and resistance to change among executives, that company will not survive in a high-speed, global marketplace. Innovation is the key to prosperity. And experimentation is the key to innovation. Order and flexibility worked together to create an increasingly effective and profitable organization at Intel.

Once Intel decided to get out of the computer memory business, it faced the question of what sort of product it would produce. Here is where timing and execution played a significant part. You will remember that I defined execution as "taking appropriate action at an appropriate time." Intel had been making 386 microprocessor chips for IBM PCs, but had not devoted significant resources to this product. At this moment, Grove irrevocably devoted his entire company's future to building microprocessors. Microprocessors were a product the Japanese could not copy easily. Further, by using a continuous product obsolescence strategy with its processor chips, Intel could assure itself of a major share of the processor market on a continuing basis at a premium profit. I am sure that it costs no more, maybe even less, to manufacture a Pentium (586) processor than it does a 386 chip.

Intel is continuously developing faster and faster chips. The company actively promotes a "latest is greatest" attitude among computer buyers, a sort of "my chip is bigger than your chip" mentality, to create demand for its newer, faster products. And the strategy works very well. Changing Intel's core business from memory to microprocessors was an appropriate action at an appropriate time. Grove's actions are an excellent case study in the proper application of Musashi's concepts.

BILL GATES — MICROSOFT

Let's continue our discussion of Musashi's tactics applied to high-technology competition. Bill Gates and Microsoft are facing a crisis during the time that this book is being written (early 1998). The United States government is accusing Microsoft of violations of the antitrust laws. So, rather than restate how Gates and his company found fame and fortune fueled by pizza and soda pop, I would like to pose some questions about strategy and tactics related to this crisis. We will place ourselves in Musashi's position, apply his reasoning, and inquire about what Mr. Gates should be doing. (The readers of this section will have an advantage over me. The strategies used and their outcomes will already be known.)

As everyone is aware, Bill Gates, founder and CEO of Microsoft and one of the world's richest men, had at least one magnificent revelation in his life. He foresaw the personal computer revolution. Further, Gates had, and continues to apply, one magnificently profitable business strategy. Simply put, his strategy for Microsoft is to create and maintain a monopoly in operating software. His early MS-DOS (DOS means "disk operating software") for IBM personal computers, along with its product descendants, Windows, Windows 95, and Windows 98, dominate the world of operating software. Microsoft products are reportedly installed on 80 percent of the world's IBM PC-based systems.

Gates pioneered the now common strategy of making computer manufacturers dependent on his software. This is an example of Musashi's principle of concentration carried to its extreme. When the microcomputer revolution began, Gates was one of many software developers supplying product to the several hundred startup microcomputer manufacturers. Through intense effort and aggressive marketing, coupled with high product suitability, MS-DOS took over the operating system market. Gates later solidified his monopoly and increased his cash flow by forcing computer manufacturers to pay him just for the privilege of having his product available on their machines. Since his software was an absolute necessity in order for computer manufacturers to sell their product, his highly focused strategy worked well. Everyone paid, but he did not make many friends.

This part of the history of Bill Gates and Microsoft is familiar to most people, so let's fast forward now to 1998. Bill is still pursuing his simple, heretofore effective strategy, but this time with his Internet browser. (An Internet browser is a software program that allows you to look at Web pages on the World Wide Web. It is the functional equivalent of operating software, except it is for the Internet.) The problem is that Mr. Gates is trying to create another monopoly, at least according to the federal government and his competitors. His first monopoly happened naturally, a result of the birth of a new technology. No one knew at the time that it was happening. The current Internet monopoly is being pursued on purpose. It is a deliberate attempt to create a money-printing machine for Microsoft.

No one (particularly Musashi and I) should criticize Bill for trying. After all, as I said earlier, the object of winning in business competition is to win *big*. The question I have is whether this tactic, which everyone — including the federal government — is prepared to fight, is the best one for Microsoft at this point. Look at the amount of time already wasted and the volume of negative press generated by the effort.

Bill should use the REACT acronym to analyze his situation to find a tactic that works. Microsoft has an immense pool of resources which it can apply to solving any problem or fighting any battle. But the business and political environment is adamantly opposed to the formation of another Microsoft monopoly. Instead of taking the attitude that Microsoft must dominate every market, why not take the opposite attitude and foster competition while maintaining an important stake in the outcomes of different technologies which are directed at profiting from emerging opportunities (for example, the Internet). Concentrate Microsoft resources into developing alternative solutions which will then stand on their own merits as products.

This approach requires a confident mindset and tolerance for risk taking. But I am sure that the employees at Microsoft can handle the challenge. People I talk to do not object to Microsoft products. They *do* object to having Microsoft products shoved down their throats. Given a reasonable choice, they may very well select Microsoft because the company can presumably produce better products.

And the time is now. The birth of every major industry in America has been accompanied by attempts by early industry executives to monopolize it. Look at the railroad industry, the steel industry, the electric power industry, the telephone industry. And here comes Microsoft. Every one of these industries has gone through extended periods of profit difficulty as a result of trying to create and foster its monopolies.

Musashi advises us to react to the reality of the situation in order to maintain our competitive balance. Microsoft has many, many high-profit opportunities. Perhaps the company should select a set of strategies and tactics which are more in tune with what seems to be the reality of the moment and the spirit of the times. Musashi would ask, "Why fight a costly, embarrassing battle which the company may not win because the time and the conditions are not right?"

There is some evidence in its recent acquisitions and investments that Microsoft is taking a more productive approach. Even as I write this, Microsoft is softening the strident tone of its news releases defending the right to create a monopoly (which the company may not have). If Microsoft handles this matter correctly, it will end up with a virtual monopoly and none of the negative repercussions.

What is Bill Gates' competitive sword? Initially, it was intense personal effort and perfect timing. Bill was the right person at the right time in history to propel the PC revolution. As a corporate bureaucracy, Microsoft probably cannot sustain the personal intensity of its founder. Its competitive sword now becomes immense resources and great reputation. To use this sword, the company as a whole must identify and exploit better opportunities without scattering resources to the wind. Great success is sometimes the most difficult situation to manage.

LAWRENCE OF ARABIA

The idea of concentration in tactics is best illustrated in warfare by situations where guerrilla tactics are successfully employed against a larger and stronger enemy. Lt. Colonel T. E. Lawrence was charged with the responsibility for commanding elements of the Arab Revolt in the Middle East during World War I. Because of the nature of the Arab army, which consisted of personally brave, but poorly organized, tribal units, and because his forces were outnumbered by the Turks by perhaps 30 to 1, Lawrence had no choice but to conduct a careful guerrilla campaign. His analysis of the situation and decisions about tactics illustrate the kind of thinking required to implement Musashi's principles effectively.

Lawrence's reasoning started with the understanding that the Arab army could not hold any territory. It was too weak for defending any position. Whenever his forces were threatened, they needed to fade into the desert, "disappear like a vapor." His conclusion was that operating materiel — equipment and supplies — rather than men was more crucial to the Turkish army. They had plenty of men. But men without food or clothes or weapons or ammunition are helpless, even against a small force. So, Lawrence determined, the Arab army would attack materiel rather than men. The idea was to concentrate attacks on railroads, supplies, or equipment in such a way that Arab soldiers were exposed to little or no danger.

In his book, *Seven Pillars of Wisdom*, Lawrence said: "The decision of what was critical would always be ours. Most wars were wars of contact, both forces striving to stay in touch to avoid tactical surprise. Ours should be a war of detachment. We were to contain the enemy by the silent threat of a vast unknown desert, not disclosing ourselves until we attacked. The attack might be nominal, directed not against him, but against his stuff; so it would seek neither his strength nor his weakness, but his most accessible material. In railway-cutting it would usually be an empty stretch of rail; and the more empty, the greater the tactical success.

"We might develop the rule never to engage the enemy, never afford them a target. Many Turks on our front had no chance all the war to fire upon us, and we were never on the defensive except by accident and in error. The corollary of such a rule was perfect intelligence, so that we could plan in certainty. The chief agent must be the general's head; and his understanding must be faultless, leaving no room for chance. Morale is built on knowledge and broken by ignorance. When we knew all about the enemy we should be comfortable."

In competitive situations, the critical elements are time and talent. To succeed, time and talent must be aligned precisely, with information as the guide, on targets which produce sufficient profit (i.e., the Warren Buffett approach to investment strategy). Attacks on competitors must be efficient, that is, low cost. Attacks must be timely. If you can occupy a competitor's critical resources (time and talent) with unproductive tasks, then you can gain a local advantage. The main requirement of this strategy is accurate, reliable, current information. You, as executive in charge, must know what the competition is doing now.

Operations based on unfounded speculation increase the risk of failure. Aligning your strength on your opponent's weakness gives you immense leverage. If you get enough leverage, you can win. Just like Lawrence eventually did.

DONALD TRUMP

Leverage is a concept which is clearly understood by Donald Trump. Trump, unlike Bill Gates and T. E. Lawrence, is not a private person. He has chosen to exhibit a high profile, to "Trump-et" his successes and failures in the world media. The publicity provides him with powerful business leverage. He has, in addition, shown himself to be a resilient fighter and superb competitor.

Trump has successfully adapted Musashi's concepts, using them in his own fashion to create and maintain his personal fortune. In his recently published memoir, *Trump: The Art of the Comeback* (Random House, New York, 1997), he gives his views on competitive strategy and tactics which I discuss below. These views parallel Musashi's principles and show how Musashi's ideas can be applied in an intensely competitive environment.

Musashi teaches that practice and preparation are essential for competitive success. In the same vein, Trump advises that "having money, good looks, and connections is a wonderful thing and certainly very important, but if you do not know what you're doing, money, looks, and connections will not solve your problems. There is an old saying that if you put a lot into something, chances are, you will get a lot out of it. While there's nothing fancy or pretty about it, plain old hard work is, with very few exceptions, a primary ingredient for attaining success. You can coax luck into your life by working hard."

Like Musashi, Trump firmly advocates the philosophy of ordered flexibility. Maintain order by grasping current reality. Remain flexible by planning for the future. Trump states that "in order to succeed, you really have to focus on the present. My policy is to learn from the past, focus on the present, and plan for the future. One thing that has become clear to me in the past few years is that you've got to be flexible and open-minded. That's part of what vision is all about — finding creative ways to make the best of both good and bad situations. I never got attached to one deal or one approach. I keep a lot of balls in the air because most deals fall out no matter how promising they seem at first."

Napoleon once said that a tree without branches will bear no fruit. Plans which are limited to one alternative often fail due to lack of flexibility. Keep multiple options available.

Competition for Donald Trump is both intense and personal. He warns, "Deals are people, they are not impersonal, and if you don't have a deep understanding of people and their motives, you can never become a great deal maker. You've got to be tough. You've got to negotiate tough, and you cannot, at any time, let anyone take advantage of you. Suddenly, the word gets out on the street that you are a pushover — or worse — and whoosh! You're history." Sword fighting is like that, too. Let down your guard for a moment and whoosh! You really are history.

Making money in real estate, gambling casinos, and hotel management is difficult at best. Trump provides insight into the fundamental aspect of succeeding in competition. He describes a situation in real-estate development as follows: "The whole thing was a mess. But where there's turmoil, there's opportunity. Timing, once again, is everything." By waiting for the appropriate moment, Trump was able to profit where others had faced only loss. Taking an appropriate action at an appropriate time is the basic skill of the master competitor.

What is Donald Trump's competitive sword? I believe his competitive sword has two edges: personal competence and public image. He uses both edges equally well. Trump is a highly competent real-estate developer. Before he became "The Donald," he proved himself by successfully developing properties in New York. He earned the trust and confidence of the financial community by making money for himself and for others. His hands-on project management skills and his ability to work with the building trade in New York allowed him to acquire and profit from opportunities. Personal competence is his first advantage.

There are many personally competent people in the world. Trump magnified his personal competence by creating and maintaining a public image. It is difficult to tell where the public Trump ends and the private one begins. In deal making, Trump's public image gives him a terrific weapon.

Look at what he does in his books. He is not the least bit hesitant about heaping praise or blame on people that have either helped or hurt him, as the case may be. His praise is effusive; his blame, scathing. If you were entering a business deal, knowing his propensity for publicly airing other people's faults, what would you be thinking? I would certainly be very worried that I might end up as a nasty footnote on page 122 of his next book. Does this give him an advantage? Possibly. As Musashi says, anything that upsets your opponent and causes him to lose his balance will help you.

Trump is a master of using Musashi's ideas about competence and confidence presented as Chapter 2 (the Foundation chapter). He uses competence to make sure that his deals work out profitably. He uses confidence to build a public image which gives him leverage going into deal negotiation. These strategies are extremely effective for him.

RORKE'S DRIFT

The British army's invasion of Zululand in 1879 set the stage for the small, but intense, Battle of Rorke's

Drift. This ferocious battle teaches the benefits of training, practice, and discipline coupled with sound assessment of the competitive situation, particularly when one is caught in some very bad circumstances. The battle is a clinic on how to apply strength against weakness to succeed in situations where the odds are really against you.

The Battle of Rorke's Drift may be the most famous battle ever fought by British soldiers of the Victorian era. It occurred shortly after the main column of British troops was attacked by the Zulu army at Isandlwana (which was about 5 miles away) and suffered an embarrassing defeat. Three thousand or more Zulu warriors, who had been part of the reserve forces at the Battle of Isandlwana, moved against the supply depot at Rorke's Drift, which was manned by 150 British troops. Outnumbered at least 20 to 1, the British troops were nonetheless able to withstand repeated massed assaults by the Zulus and hold their position from the afternoon of January 22, 1879 until the morning of January 23 when the Zulu army retreated.

At first glance, it may seem that the British force stood no chance against the overwhelming numerical superiority of the Zulu force. But the British side had some significant strengths. First, they had better weapons and virtually unlimited ammunition. The main attack weapon of the Zulu army was a short stabbing spear which could only be used at short range. The Zulus also had a number of rifles and guns.

But because the warriors were not trained to use them effectively and they had no proper powder or bullets, the guns could not give them any additional impact. The British had modern rifles accurate at ranges of 500 yards. Further, Rorke's Drift was a supply depot. The defenders had lots of bullets.

Second, the British prepared a strong defensive position. Walls built of biscuit boxes, meal bags, and overturned wagons gave them a solid defensive perimeter. With a bayonet attached, the British rifle was much longer than the Zulu stabbing spear, the tribe's primary weapon for centuries. This meant that the Zulu warriors had to attack by first running through several hundred yards of accurate rifle fire; then they had to go over the walls which were manned by desperate soldiers armed with bayonets which could reach a greater distance than their own spears. Although the British were forced to reduce the size of their defensive perimeter during the fight, the wall was never breached.

Third, and most important, the British were trained to fight this kind of engagement and had the military discipline to hold up under pressure. The two officers in charge of the depot on the day of the battle, Lieutenants John Chard, an engineer, and Gonville Bromhead, an infantry officer, did not have distinguished records. Chard had not seen action before. They did, however, have years of British army training and discipline. They and their men had a long tradition of order and performance under fire. Once the two officers realized their difficult position, they knew exactly what to do. And they did it. I believe they must have had confidence in their ability to defend this post against the threat.

The British survived the Battle of Rorke's Drift because they followed Musashi's fundamental principle of concentrating strength against weakness. Superior weapons and superior position, coupled with effective execution, made the difference. The Zulus did not make good use of their numerical advantage, choosing to waste men and energy in brave, but uncoordinated, attacks.

COMMON THREADS

In researching the exploits of the master competitors I discuss above, I have observed common threads in their lives and in how they handle competitive situations. Each of these competitors applies the heart of Musashi's philosophy, which can be boiled down to three short statements:

1. Prepare always.
2. Recognize reality.
3. Take action.

These competitors share some common characteristics and experiences:

1. They do not succeed every time. But they do not stop trying and they do learn from their mistakes.
2. They emphasize their strengths, not their weaknesses. Each person is very strong in applying some of the seven principles of competitive success, but is not necessarily expert at all of them.
3. They have a high tolerance for random events and understand, at least intuitively, the effects of probability on the outcome of their actions. They exploit probability by aligning strength where it will do the most good.

I do not believe that success in competitive situations is a mere matter of chance. Clearly, preparation, analysis, and action play important parts. Opportunity abounds in the wired world of tomorrow. But there are many people pursuing that opportunity. Without a strong foundation in the principles of winning in competition, your ability to obtain power, position, and prestige are diminished. Learn Musashi's principles. Use them for your benefit.

All the situations discussed above where the weaker force defeated or withstood attacks by the stronger force are exceptions to the general rule of competition: most of the time, in competition, whether military or business, the stronger side wins. When you have great resources at your disposal, it is easy to assume that you can win in every situation because you usually do. But in the rapidly evolving wired marketplaces of the twenty-first century, any kind of complacency will sooner or later lead to loss. The computer network which exists throughout the world allows swift and convenient exchange of information about prices and services. Competitors can literally pop up overnight. Small, lean, concentrated companies can be fierce competitors. So can lean, concentrated larger companies.

THE WAY OF THE MASTER COMPETITOR

Musashi's principles are a reliable, solid framework for competitive thinking, regardless of the competitive situation. Working through the seven principles of competitive success — each business day, as you make decisions — will keep important factors up front. When a competitive challenge occurs, you will be ready. Here is a quick review of Musashi's competitive principles for business executives.

MUSASHI'S PRINCIPLES

1. Ordered flexibility
2. Execution
3. Resources
4. Environment
5. Attitude
6. Concentration
7. Timing

1. Ordered flexibility is the fundamental philosophical tenet of Musashi's entire approach to winning in conflicts. It embodies preparation, observation, poise, timing, and readiness to act. That is, the competitive executive is prepared to do whatever is necessary given the actual situation. He is grounded in the reality of the moment, observant and poised. Yet, he can easily respond to changing circumstances. He does not make up his mind to act until the appropriate time, but when he does act, he moves decisively. The objective of ordered flexibility is to allow the executive to determine the most appropriate response to opportunity or challenge.

2. Execution means getting the job done, applying tactics to circumstances. Once competitors have determined where they will align resources and created a plan of action, the plan must be carried out successfully in order to get the benefits. Several factors should be considered in execution. They are: resources, environment, attitude, concentration, and timing.

3. Resources are the assets you have available. The most significant of these is people. The right people must be in the right place. Action depends on people. In a critical situation, the difference between success and failure is the competence of the person on the spot. Capable, trained people must be in place before they are needed.

4. Environment is the place and situation in which a competitive situation is occurring. It could be as small as a meeting room or as large as the floor of the New York Stock Exchange. There are particular dynamics associated with every different environment. These dynamics must be understood and used to your advantage.

5. Attitude is the way you think about the competition at hand. Stupidity is not an acceptable attitude. The most effective attitude is one of ordered flexibility. The facts govern the situation. There is a reality present whether you like it or not. Pay attention to reality. Attune your senses to discover the way to win.

6. Concentration simply means focusing your strength on your opponent's weakness. Or, in an impersonal sense, concentration directs resources towards opportunity. Effective concentration is critical to success because no company or individual has unlimited resources. It is like the blade of the sword, the cutting edge of competitive tactics. Sharp concentration is a critical aspect of success in competitive situations. No person or company has enough resources to exploit every opportunity or fight every battle. Musashi says:

The ability to focus is your greatest asset in a competitive situation. When you appreciate the power of focus, you will feel the rhythm of your opponent and maintain control of his actions. You will understand his approach and effortlessly defeat him by naturally concentrating your attack in an appropriate place at an appropriate time.

7. Timing means that action must be taken at the right time. Timing determines whether an action produces desired results or produces nothing. Successful leaders know when to move and when to remain still, when to attack and when to retreat.

The seven principles of competitive thinking developed by Musashi in *The Book of Five Rings* are as effective for managing today's business situations as they have been for winning military battles. They are both easy to remember and readily applied. People who train themselves and others to use this framework during normal business operations will automatically adopt ordered flexibility during a challenge or crisis, increasing the probability of a successful outcome. Follow Musashi's principles and be a master competitor.

THE ART OF WAR
FOR EXECUTIVES
DONALD G. KRAUSE

For years, business schools and professional consultants have turned to Sun Tzu's 2500-year-old Chinese text for its invaluable commentary on such topics as leadership, strategy, organization, competition and cooperation.

Now the wisdom of Sun Tzu's *The Art of War* is made accessible to the modern reader. Not simply a new translation, this is the first book to provide a clear, easy-to-follow interpretation of the classic document. *The Art of War for Executives* reveals the brilliance of Sun Tzu – and shows how to win on the battlefield of modern business. The tone and insight of the original classic remain, while incorporating the ideas of contemporary business philosophers like Peters, Drucker and Bennis.

Sun Tzu's ten principles for competitive success are:

- Learn to fight
- Do it right
- Expect the worst
- Burn the bridges
- Pull together

- Show the way
- Know the facts
- Seize the day
- Do it better
- Keep them guessing

Here at last is an accessible interpretation of Sun Tzu's *The Art of War* incorporating modern business lessons to make this classic text relevant and readable for today's executive facing strategic and competitive challenges.

£7.99 PB I 95788 130 3
132pp 215x138mm

THE WAY OF
THE LEADER

Donald G. Krause

The challenges to leadership are not new, nor are they unique to modern times. The rulers of ancient China spent a great deal of time studying and thinking about leadership, particularly leadership under conditions of great difficulty – the change, chaos and uncertainty caused by war, famine and social upheaval. Taken together, the leadership concepts of two men in particular – the famous general Sun Tzu and the great philosopher Confucius – outline a system for effective leadership that has worked for centuries even under the worst possible conditions.

The Way of the Leader brings the philosophical vision of *The Art of War* and *The Analects of Confucius* to the bottom line. Donald Krause organizes and integrates business-related adaptations of these two classics with the best ideas of modern military and political leaders. In so doing he creates a clear and understandable framework for effective leadership that can be used successfully by individuals and organizations in today's competitive international business environment.

The Way of the Leader is designed to be a schematic for victory, a road map to success. By using the ideas of Sun Tzu and Confucius, in conjunction with effective management practices, you can and will become a better business leader.

£7.99 PB 1 95788 137 0
196pp 215x138mm

ORDER FORM

Titles are available from all good bookshops, OR SEND YOUR COMPLETED ORDER TO:

Nicholas Brealey Publishing Ltd   Tel: +44 (0)171 430 0224
36 John Street   *Fax: +44 (0)171 404 8311*
London WC1A 2AT   http://www.nbrealey-books.com
UK

Title	ISBN	Price	Qty	Cost
		Subtotal		
Postage (UK or surface mail outside the UK)				£2.95
OR Postage Airmail (add £8.00 and delete £2.95 above)				
			TOTAL	

BY CHEQUE:

I enclose a cheque (payable to Nicholas Brealey Publishing) for £.........

BY CREDIT CARD:

I authorise you to debit my credit card account for £.........
My Mastercard/Visa/American Express/Diners Club card number is:

Expiry date:................. Tel no:........................
Cardholder's name: .... Signature: ....
Position: .... Organization:...................
Address:................... Postcode:.....................
Pro Forma Invoices issued on request: Please tick ☐
Bulk order discounts are available.   Please call +44 (0)171 430 0224